Manufacturing on the Move

# MANUFACTURING
## *on the*
# MOVE

*Robert W. Crandall*

**The Brookings Institution**
*Washington, D.C.*

Copyright © 1993

THE BROOKINGS INSTITUTION

1775 Massachusetts Avenue, N.W., Washington, D.C. 20036

Library of Congress Cataloging-in-Publication data:

Crandall, Robert W.
    Manufacturing on the move / Robert W. Crandall.
        p.    cm.
    Includes bibliographical references and index.
    ISBN 0–8157–1598–6 (cloth)—ISBN 0–8157–1597–8 (pbk.)
    1. United States—Manufactures. 2. Lake States—Manufactures.
3. United States—Economic conditions—1981– —Regional disparities. 4. Industrial productivity—United States—Regional disparities. I. Title.
HD9725.C68 1993
338.4'767'0973—dc20                                                        92-43320
                                                                                                  CIP


9  8  7  6  5  4  3  2  1


The paper used in this publication meets the minimum requirements of the
American National Standard for Information Sciences—Permanence of paper for
Printed Library Materials, ANSI Z39.48–1984

# THE BROOKINGS INSTITUTION

The Brookings Institution is an independent organization devoted to nonpartisan research, education, and publication in economics, government, foreign policy, and the social sciences generally. Its principal purposes are to aid in the development of sound public policies and to promote public understanding of issues of national importance.

The Institution was founded on December 8, 1927, to merge the activities of the Institute for Government Research, founded in 1916, the Institute of Economics, founded in 1922, and the Robert Brookings Graduate School of Economics and Government, founded in 1924.

The Board of Trustees is responsible for the general administration of the Institution, while the immediate direction of the policies, program, and staff is vested in the President, assisted by an advisory committee of the officers and staff. The by-laws of the Institution state: "It is the function of the Trustees to make possible the conduct of scientific research, and publication, under the most favorable conditions, and to safeguard the independence of the research staff in the pursuit of their studies and in the publication of the results of such studies. It is not a part of their function to determine, control, or influence the conduct of particular investigations or the conclusions reached."

The President bears final responsibility for the decision to publish a manuscript as a Brookings book. In reaching his judgment on the competence, accuracy, and objectivity of each study, the President is advised by the director of the appropriate research program and weighs the views of a panel of expert outside readers who report to him in confidence on the quality of the work. Publication of a work signifies that it is deemed a competent treatment worthy of public consideration but does not imply endorsement of conclusions or recommendations.

The Institution maintains its position of neutrality on issues of public policy in order to safeguard the intellectual freedom of the staff. Hence interpretations or conclusions in Brookings publications should be understood to be solely those of the authors and should not be attributed to the Institution, to its trustees, officers, or other staff members, or to the organizations that support its research.

# Foreword

In the 1970s and 1980s, competition buffeted many basic American industries. At first, imports of automobiles, heavy equipment, machine tools, rubber tires, ball bearings, and steel placed severe strains on the established firms in these industries. Later, new plants, built by both foreign and new domestic competitors, continued this assault on the older, established U.S. producers. However, the new domestic competitors located in the South and West, rather than in the older Rust Belt regions of the United States. As a result, the number of high-wage northern jobs fell.

In this book, Robert Crandall examines the shift of manufacturing from the northern Rust Belt areas—the states stretching from New York to Wisconsin. Differences in labor market conditions—wage rates and the degree of unionization—are the primary explanation for the growth of new manufacturing establishments in the South and West. He provides new evidence that the migration is not likely to stop, because these differences have not narrowed. With a shrinking supply of new high-paid, unionized, manufacturing jobs in the northern areas of the country, opportunities for new unskilled workers entering the labor force have narrowed.

Crandall concludes that the government can do little to stop this migration. He suggests that reduced regulatory costs, targeted wage subsidies in areas with persistent unemployment, and incentives for education and training are most likely to improve the local environment for new manufacturing investment.

Robert Crandall is a senior fellow in the Economic Studies program at Brookings. He acknowledges the assistance of Bruce Phillips of the Small Business Administration, who provided data and technical advice. Helpful suggestions were received from Timothy J. Bartik, Robert E. Litan, Mancur Olson, and Leonard F. Wheat.

Research assistance was provided by Jonathan Galst, Christopher Owen, Dawn Senecal, and Stephanie Wilshusen.

Funding for this project was provided by the Brookings Center for Economic Progress and Employment, whose supporters comprise Donald S. Perkins; Aetna Life and Casualty Company; American Express Philanthropic Program; AT&T Foundation; The Ford Foundation; Ford Motor Company Fund; General Electric Foundation; Hewlett-Packard Company; Institute for International Economic Studies; Morgan Stanley & Co., Inc.; Motorola Foundation; The Prudential Foundation; Springs Industries, Inc.; The Starr Foundation; Union Carbide Corporation; Alex C. Walker Educational and Charitable Foundation; Warner-Lambert Company; and Xerox Corporation.

Nancy D. Davidson edited the manuscript, and David Bearce verified its factual content. David Rossetti provided staff assistance, Susan L. Woollen prepared the manuscript for typesetting, and Florence Robinson prepared the index.

The views expressed in this book are those of the author and should not be ascribed to those persons or organizations whose assistance is acknowledged or to the trustees, officers, or other staff members of the Brookings Institution.

BRUCE K. MACLAURY
*President*

*Washington, D.C.*
*April 1990*

# Contents

Tables

# Figures

# Manufacturing on the Move

# U.S. Census Divisions and Regions

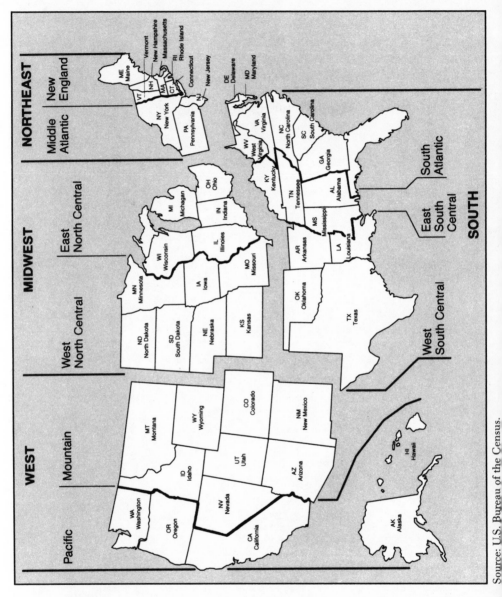

Source: U.S. Bureau of the Census.

*Chapter One*

# Regional Changes in Population and Production

THROUGHOUT THE 1980s one of the major concerns of domestic policymakers was that the United States was "deindustrializing." Politicians, labor leaders, and industrialists in the Rust Belt states—the band of states extending west from New York and New Jersey through Wisconsin—were particularly worried. Even if the entire country was not deindustrializing, there was surely evidence that the northeastern and Great Lakes states were. Abandoned factories in Buffalo, Pittsburgh, Youngstown, Detroit, and Milwaukee were ample testimony to the decline in northern manufacturing.

The popular explanation for the decline in these industrial regions was the slow economic growth after the oil shocks of the 1970s and the sharp rise in the dollar that occurred in the early 1980s.[1] Both of these explanations seem dated by 1993. The United States enjoyed eight years of sustained economic growth after the 1982 recession, and by 1992 the dollar had receded to its lowest real level since the early 1970s. If the lack of growth and an overvalued dollar were the causes of the Rust Belt's problems in 1980–85, surely this area should have recovered since 1985. But manufacturing employment in these states continues to decline, and jobs continue to shift to the South and West.

In this volume, I examine the causes of the divergent trends in regional manufacturing growth in the United States and the consequences of these trends for individual well-being in each region. I try to predict whether the shift of output to the South and West

1. See, for example, William H. Branson and James P. Love, "The Real Exchange Rate and Employment in U.S. Manufacturing: State and Regional Results," Working Paper 2435 (Cambridge, Mass.: National Bureau of Economic Research, November 1987).

**Table 1-1. Migration in Regional Population Growth, Selected Periods, 1960–90[a]**

Thousands unless otherwise indicated

| Region | 1960–70 | | 1970–80 | | 1980–85 | | 1985–90 | | Annual rate of growth (percent) | |
| --- | --- | --- | --- | --- | --- | --- | --- | --- | --- | --- |
| | Net change[b] | Net migration[c] | Net change[b] | Net migration[c] | Net change[b] | Net migration[c] | Net change[b] | Net migration[c] | 1960–70 | 1970–90 |
| New England | 1,338 | 316 | 501 | –241 | 313 | 28 | 723 | 37 | 1.2 | 0.5 |
| Middle Atlantic | 3,034 | 59 | –426 | –2,647 | 412 | –355 | 529 | –658 | 0.9 | 0.1 |
| East north central | 4,028 | –153 | 1,419 | –2,220 | –6 | –1,462 | 725 | –455 | 1.1 | 0.2 |
| West north central | 930 | –599 | 856 | –484 | 362 | –276 | 337 | –9 | 0.6 | 0.4 |
| South Atlantic | 4,700 | 1,332 | 6,280 | 3,440 | 3,255 | 2,090 | 3,455 | 1,885 | 1.7 | 1.8 |
| East south central | 754 | –698 | 1,858 | 556 | 459 | –32 | 286 | 86 | 0.6 | 0.8 |
| West south central | 2,371 | –42 | 4,421 | 1,995 | 2,781 | 1,399 | 591 | –457 | 1.3 | 1.6 |
| Mountain | 1,429 | 307 | 3,083 | 1,730 | 1,393 | 612 | 916 | 89 | 1.9 | 2.5 |
| Pacific | 5,328 | 2,547 | 5,251 | 2,385 | 3,220 | 1,541 | 3,985 | 1,502 | 2.3 | 1.9 |
| Northeastern[d] | 8,400 | 222 | 1,494 | –5,108 | 719 | –1,789 | 1,977 | –1,076 | 1.0 | 0.2 |
| Rest of country | 15,512 | –2,847 | 21,749 | 9,622 | 11,470 | 5,334 | 9,570 | 3,116 | 1.5 | 1.6 |

Sources: Bureau of the Census, *Statistical Abstract of the United States, 1980,* 101st ed. (Department of Commerce, 1980), p. 13; *Statistical Abstract, 1989,* 109th ed. (1989), p. 21; *Statistical Abstract, 1990,* 110th ed. (1990), p. 22; *Statistical Abstract, 1992,* 112th ed. (1992), p. 22; and Bureau of the Census, "Geographical Mobility: March 1987 to March 1990," *Current Population Reports,* series P-20, no. 456 (Department of Commerce, 1991), pp. 82, 248.

a. All data are for April 1 except 1985 and 1990, which are measured on July 1.
b. Overall change in population due to deaths, births, and migration.
c. Difference between immigration from other states and other countries and emigration to this region.
d. New England, middle Atlantic, and east north central.

will continue in the decades ahead. Finally, I attempt to determine if there are policy instruments that could affect the regional composition of industrial output.


## Population and Incomes

Since 1960 the U.S. population has increased from 180 million to more than 250 million, growing at a rate of about 1 percent a year. However, the distribution of this growth has been quite uneven. In the cold, industrial northeastern regions of the country population growth has slowed to a crawl. As a result, the geographic center of the U.S. population has moved more rapidly to the South and West in the past thirty years than in earlier decades of this century.[2]

Even as late as the 1960s, the northeastern states' population was growing at a rate of 1 percent a year, or approximately two-thirds the national average (table 1-1), but in the late 1960s this growth began to ebb. Since 1970 these northeastern states have grown by less than 0.2 percent a year while the remainder of the country has experienced population growth of 1.6 percent a year.

Much of the difference in regional growth rates has been caused by a surge in migration to the South and West that began in the late 1960s and accelerated markedly in the 1970s. Between 1970 and 1980 alone, net outmigration from the middle Atlantic and east north central (Great Lakes) regions totaled 4.9 million, or about 6 percent of their 1970 population (table 1-1). Although the migration from these two regions moderated somewhat in the 1980s, a net flow of population continued from the North to the South and West, particularly to the southeastern and western coastal states.[3]

The outmigration from the west north central region—the area from Minnesota and North Dakota in the north to Kansas and Missouri in the south—is obviously a reflection of the declining U.S. farm population. But the migration out of the northeastern indus-

2. Bureau of the Census, *1980 Census of Population* (Department of Commerce, 1982), vol. 1, chap. A.

3. More recent data show a continuing outmigration of about 300,000 persons a year from the northeastern states since 1988, but only 50,000 a year from the midwestern states. Bureau of the Census, "Geographical Mobility: March 1987 to March 1990," *Current Population Reports*, series P-20, no. 456 (Department of Commerce, 1991).

**Table 1-2. Regional per Capita Income as Percentage of U.S. Average, Selected Years, 1959–89**

| Region | 1959 | 1969 | 1979 | 1989 |
|---|---|---|---|---|
| New England | 109 | 110 | 103 | 120 |
| Middle Atlantic | 115 | 113 | 105 | 115 |
| East north central | 107 | 105 | 105 | 99 |
| West north central | 92 | 93 | 100 | 94 |
| South Atlantic | 84 | 90 | 92 | 97 |
| East south central | 68 | 73 | 79 | 79 |
| West south central | 83 | 83 | 94 | 84 |
| Mountain | 94 | 89 | 94 | 88 |
| Pacific | 118 | 115 | 112 | 108 |

Source: Data from Department of Commerce, Bureau of Economic Analysis, Regional Economic Information System (September 1992).

trial regions—the primary concern of this volume—is surely caused by something else.

The obvious candidates for explaining the exodus from the northern industrial regions are economic: as industries decline, people migrate to improve their economic status. But average incomes have always been higher in the Northeast than in the South. In 1960 the average per capita income in the three northeastern census regions was approximately 19 percent above the average in the South and West. Thirty years later the gap was still about 14 percent.[4]

If incomes are higher in the North, why would people move southward in search of economic rewards?[5] If wages—adjusted for skill levels—are indeed higher in the North, it is capital that would be expected to move southward, reducing the demand for labor and wages in the North and bidding up wages in the South relative to those in the North, and thus narrow the North-South income differentials. Census data on per capita income do show a gradual narrowing of regional differences in income between 1959 and 1979, years of roughly equivalent macroeconomic performance (see table 1-2). However, the 1980s witnessed a reversal of this trend in the

4. Data from Department of Commerce, Bureau of Economic Analysis. In chapter 2, I review the recent literature on economic convergence and its relevance to industrial migration.

5. Mancur Olson, "The South Will Fall Again: The South as Leader and Laggard in Economic Growth," *Southern Economic Journal*, vol. 49 (April 1983), pp. 917–32, asks this question provocatively and offers an answer that is quite consistent with the results in chapter 2.

New England and middle Atlantic regions, and by 1989 the North-east's relative per capita incomes were at or above even their 1959 levels. Moreover, the west south central states receded back to their 1959 relative level while the mountain and Pacific states fell below their 1959 standing.

There are some obvious explanations for the recidivism in regional income distribution in the 1980s. The financial and real estate booms were much stronger in the Northeast than in the industrial heartland or the South. The energy boom collapsed in the Southwest and the mountain states. But there may be other, more fundamental structural impediments to closing the regional income disparities despite population and industrial migration.

For instance, there could be some barriers to the regional movement of capital or labor or market imperfections that prevent factor incomes from equalizing across states. But there are no obvious barriers to capital mobility,[6] and there has been substantial labor mobility. There may, however, be market imperfections that keep wages from being bid down in some industries in the North or that prevent southern and western firms from competing with higher-wage northern firms in these industries.

An alternative explanation is that the quality of life in the South or West has been improving relative to that available in the North. However, if it were the ambience of these Sun Belt locations that was attracting workers, one would expect to find a tightening of labor markets in the Northeast and a slackening of labor markets in the South and West. If, on the other hand, capital were moving to the South or West in search of lower-cost labor, one would expect unemployment to rise in the Northeast and to decline in the South and West while relative wages moved in the opposite direction.

There is no doubt that goods production has moved steadily to the South and West. In the next chapter, I shall investigate the role of relative wage rates in this migration, but for the present it is sufficient to note that manufacturing wage rates in the two major northeastern census regions—the middle Atlantic and east north central regions—have remained substantially above the national average for the past three decades despite the shift of employment to

6. Government regulation, particularly environmental regulation, may impede capital mobility in some industries. See Robert W. Crandall, *Controlling Industrial Pollution: The Economics and Politics of Clean Air* (Brookings, 1983).

**Figure 1-1. Unemployment Rates, Selected Regions, 1970-91**

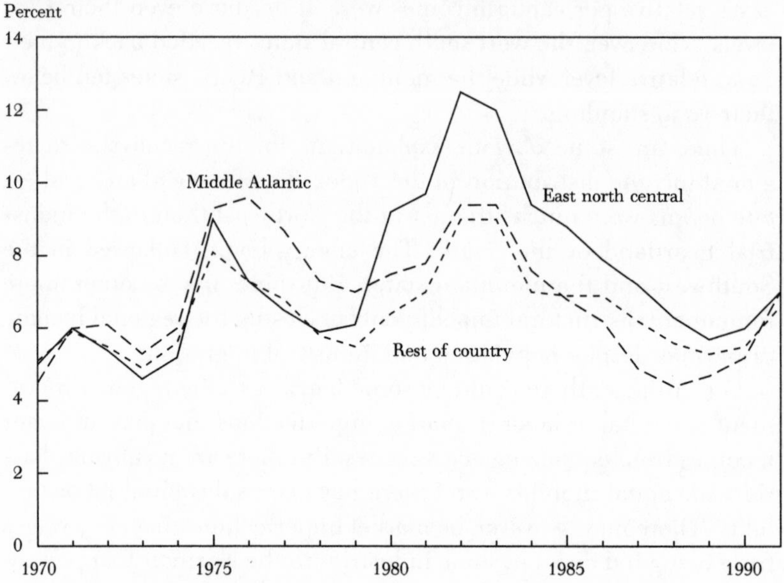

Percent

Source: Department of Labor, Bureau of Labor Statistics, Local Area Unemployment Statistics data.

the South and West. At the same time, however, average unemployment rates in these two northern regions have generally been above the national average (figure 1-1).

A recent paper by Olivier Blanchard and Lawrence Katz sheds some light on the dynamics of unemployment, labor migration, and wage rates.[7] They find that periodic unfavorable labor-demand shocks in the North create lengthy periods of substantial unemployment but much less downward movement in wages. The spells of unemployment, in turn, induce workers to migrate to the growing regions of the country, contracting labor supply in the North and eventually reestablishing labor-market equilibrium at a wage that is very close to the pre-shock level.

This process, repeated over successive oil shocks, exchange rate changes, and recessions in the 1970s and early 1980s, resulted in a narrowing of North-South income differentials. In the mid–1980s these income differentials grew once again as labor markets in the North tightened in response to the construction boom and the de-

7. Olivier Jean Blanchard and Lawrence F. Katz, "Regional Evolutions," *Brookings Papers on Economic Activity, 1992:1*, pp. 1–75.

cline in the dollar. Throughout this entire period, however, manufacturing employment continued to grow more rapidly in the South and West than in the North, and the regional structure of manufacturing wages remained essentially unchanged.[8]

## Regional Output Trends

The westward and southward shift in population has been accompanied by (if not caused by) a similar shift in economic activity. Given that labor income accounts for a large share of the factor income from overall economic activity, these coincident trends are hardly surprising. Consistent estimates of total economic output by individual states ("gross state output") are available from the Department of Commerce only for the period since 1963.[9] These data show much more sluggish growth during 1963–89 in the middle Atlantic and east north central regions than in the South and West. Surprisingly, New England actually exhibits a small increase in its share of national output over this period (see table 1-3).[10]

The east north central region's share of national output declined more rapidly than its population share between 1963 and 1989, resulting in a decline in its average per capita income relative to the rest of the country. By contrast, the decline in the other two northeastern regions' share of output was slower than their loss of population, resulting in a rise in their per capita incomes relative to the rest of the country.

For manufacturing output, the regional pattern is quite different. It shifted much more dramatically southward and westward than did overall output during 1963–89. The middle Atlantic and east north central regions' combined share of manufacturing output declined by nearly 30 percent, while the South and West enjoyed a combined increase of 33 percent in their share. The New England

8. See tables 1-7 and 4-2 below.

9. For more recent gross state product estimates, see Edward A. Trott, Jr., Ann E. Dunbar, and Howard L. Friedenberg, "Gross State Product by Industry, 1977–89," *Survey of Current Business*, vol. 71 (December 1991), pp. 43–59.

10. Since 1989 New England has been in a deep recession. Its share of personal income fell by 0.3 percentage point from 1989 through the second quarter of 1992, which suggests that its share of gross state output had returned to roughly its 1960s level.

**Table 1-3. Share of U.S. Population, Gross State Output, and Manufacturing Output, by Region, Selected Years, 1963–89**
Percent

| Year | New England | Middle Atlantic | East north central | South | West |
|---|---|---|---|---|---|
| *Population* | | | | | |
| 1963 | 5.8 | 18.9 | 19.8 | 30.9 | 16.3 |
| 1969 | 5.8 | 18.4 | 19.8 | 31.2 | 17.0 |
| 1979 | 5.5 | 16.4 | 18.5 | 33.1 | 18.8 |
| 1989 | 5.3 | 15.2 | 17.0 | 34.5 | 20.9 |
| *Gross state output* | | | | | |
| 1963 | 5.6 | 19.6 | 20.6 | 27.6 | 18.9 |
| 1969 | 5.6 | 19.3 | 20.4 | 29.0 | 18.4 |
| 1979 | 5.1 | 16.1 | 18.8 | 31.8 | 20.7 |
| 1989 | 6.0 | 16.4 | 16.7 | 31.9 | 22.1 |
| *Gross state manufacturing output* | | | | | |
| 1963 | 6.7 | 22.5 | 30.1 | 21.1 | 13.9 |
| 1969 | 6.5 | 21.3 | 29.9 | 22.8 | 13.5 |
| 1979 | 6.1 | 17.2 | 27.0 | 27.4 | 15.3 |
| 1989 | 6.5 | 15.4 | 22.3 | 28.9 | 17.9 |

Source: Data from Department of Commerce, Bureau of Economic Analysis, Regional Economic Information System (September 1992), Regional Economic Analysis Division (November 1991).

states roughly held their share through 1989, but their manufacturing sector has since declined precipitously.[11]

It is clear, therefore, that the decline of the Rust Belt states is heavily concentrated in manufacturing. In the middle Atlantic states, other sectors—such as construction, real estate, and finance—offset the loss in manufacturing through 1989, but in the states around the Great Lakes the sharp decline in manufacturing has not been cushioned by offsetting increases in other sectors. Moreover, given the recent problems in the financial and construction sectors, it is likely that the middle Atlantic region's apparent resilience may be short lived.

## Manufacturing

My principal concern here is the regional shift in manufacturing output and employment away from the Rust Belt—an area that

11. Manufacturing employment in New England fell by about 15 percent between 1989 and mid-1992. *Employment and Earnings*, various issues. Later estimates of gross state product in manufacturing are not available.

comprises the three middle Atlantic states (New York, Pennsylvania, and New Jersey) and the five states in the east north central census region (Wisconsin, Michigan, Illinois, Indiana, and Ohio). Obviously, this means that I ignore developments in about two-thirds of the private economy—mostly the service sectors. This is not an oversight for a number of reasons.

First, locational advantages are more important for manufacturing than for many service sectors. Second, the demand for the services of many sectors such as government, retailing, public utilities, personal services, and business services derives from the strength of other sectors in the immediate area, such as manufacturing, construction, or agriculture.[12] While the causation may run both ways, these service sectors are more likely to depend on local industry, not vice versa. The decline of Youngstown, Ohio, for instance, must surely be ascribed to the loss of virtually all of its steel works, which in turn has forced a contraction of other sectors. Finally, the manufacturing sector is the most important export sector for the Rust Belt and its most important source of high-paying jobs for low- and moderate-skill workers.

### National Trends

It is possible that the decline in Rust Belt manufacturing is simply a reflection of the larger problem of deindustrialization in the United States. As the United States loses comparative advantage in manufacturing—particularly in low-tech industries, the Rust Belt obviously suffers more than other regions. But it is far from clear that the United States is deindustrializing. Data developed by the Bureau of Economic Analysis (BEA) show that the real share of GNP in manufacturing, mining, construction, and electrical utilities has remained remarkably stable over the last part of the twentieth century (table 1-4). Earlier estimates of these magnitudes were criticized by Lawrence Mishel, who pointed out that the BEA's deflation procedure and periodic adjustments to the data render the

12. Regional economic analyses often refer to manufacturing, mining, agriculture, and some financial sectors as "base" industries—industries whose output is exported to other regions. See, for example, Walter Isard, *Methods of Regional Analysis: An Introduction to Regional Science* (MIT Press, 1960). For a more recent discussion, see Edward Moscovitch, "The Downturn in the New England Economy: What Lies Behind It?" *New England Economic Review* (July–August 1990), pp. 53–65.

Table 1-4. Nominal and Real Share of GNP of Industrial Sectors of the
U.S. Economy, Selected Years, 1957–89

Percent

| | Manufacturing | | Mining | | Construction | | Electrical and gas utilities[a] | | Total industry | |
|---|---|---|---|---|---|---|---|---|---|---|
| Year | N[b] | R[c] | N[b] | R[c] | N[b] | R[c] | N[b] | R[c] | N[b] | R[c] |
| 1957 | 29.8 | 20.6 | 3.1 | 3.8 | 4.7 | 4.0 | 2.3 | 2.8 | 39.9 | 31.2 |
| 1967 | 28.2 | 19.0 | 1.7 | 2.7 | 4.5 | 5.3 | 2.3 | 2.5 | 36.7 | 29.5 |
| 1977 | 23.4 | 22.5 | 2.5 | 4.9 | 4.9 | 5.3 | 2.7 | 3.4 | 33.5 | 36.1 |
| 1985 | 19.7 | 21.5 | 2.8 | 3.8 | 4.6 | 4.6 | 3.2 | 3.0 | 30.3 | 32.9 |
| 1989 | 18.6 | 22.6 | 1.5 | 3.1 | 4.8 | 4.3 | 3.0 | 3.3 | 27.9 | 33.3 |

Source: Data from Department of Commerce, Bureau of Economic Analysis, National Income and Health Division (May 6, 1991).
a. Includes electric utilities, gas utilities, and sanitary services.
b. Nominal (in current dollars).
c. Real (in constant dollars using BEA sector deflator).

conclusions of industrial stability suspect.[13] Robert Lawrence, on the other hand, argued that data on net imports and final sales support the conclusions drawn from the earlier BEA data.[14] Recent revisions by the BEA confirm that Lawrence was correct and that the real share of manufacturing in the U.S. economy has not declined.[15]

The national trend in manufacturing employment is quite different from that shown by manufacturing output. While total U.S. employment has risen steadily since the 1960s, manufacturing employment has remained mired in the range of 18 million to 20 million for the past three decades (table 1-5). Thus the *share* of total employment accounted for by manufacturing has declined steadily over the entire post-World War II period. The reason for this decline is, in part, the superior performance of manufacturing productivity over this period. Labor productivity and total factor productivity for the entire nonfarm private economy have grown much more slowly than productivity in manufacturing (table 1-6). This means that unless the demand for manufacturing output is very price elastic or

13. Lawrence Mishel, *Manufacturing Numbers: How Inaccurate Statistics Conceal U.S. Industrial Decline* (Washington: Economic Policy Institute, 1988).

14. Robert Z. Lawrence, "Issues in Measurement and International Comparison of Output Growth in Manufacturing," in Peter Hooper and J. David Richardson, eds., *International Economic Transactions: Issues in Measurement and Empirical Research* (University of Chicago Press, 1991), pp. 357–80.

15. Frank DeLeeuw, Michael Mohr, and Robert P. Parker, "Gross Product by Industry, 1977–88: A Progress Report on Improving the Estimates," *Survey of Current Business*, vol. 71 (January 1991), pp. 23–37.

**Table 1-5. Manufacturing Share of U.S. Employment, Selected Periods, 1950–89**

Employment in thousands

| Period | Average manufacturing employment | Average nonfarm employment | Manufacturing share (percent) |
|--------|--------|--------|--------|
| 1950–59 | 16,605 | 50,146 | 33.1 |
| 1960–69 | 18,092 | 60,742 | 29.8 |
| 1970–79 | 20,588 | 78,534 | 26.2 |
| 1980–89 | 19,299 | 96,893 | 19.9 |

Source: *Employment and Earnings*, May issues, various years.

**Table 1-6. Annual Productivity Growth, Selected Periods, 1960–90**

Percent

| Period | Total factor productivity | | Labor productivity | |
|--------|--------|--------|--------|--------|
| | Manufacturing | Total nonfarm | Manufacturing | Total nonfarm |
| 1960–70 | 1.7 | 1.4 | 2.8 | 2.4 |
| 1970–80 | 1.4 | 0.3 | 2.4 | 1.1 |
| 1980–90 | 3.0 | 0.7 | 2.9 | 0.9 |

Source: Data from Department of Labor, Bureau of Labor Statistics, Office of Productivity and Technology.

grows more rapidly than the demand for other goods and services, employment in manufacturing must fall relative to overall national employment.

### The Regional Distribution of Manufacturing

From the beginning of the industrial revolution in the United States until the 1960s, the northern states were the center of manufacturing activity. Indeed, from the first decade of this century through World War II, growing manufacturing industries attracted migrants from the South. Immediately after World War II, however, manufacturing began to shift from the North to the South and West. In 1947 the two Rust Belt regions accounted for 59.4 percent of U.S. value added in manufacturing, or just 3.8 percent less than in 1909. Between these two years, however, U.S. manufacturing had expanded substantially, more than trebling its total employment.[16] By 1967 these two Rust Belt regions' share of manufacturing value

16. Data from Bureau of the Census, *Census of Manufactures* (Department of Commerce, 1947), p. 33.

**Table 1-7. Manufacturing Employment, by Region, Selected Years, 1967–91**
Numbers in thousands

| Region | 1967 | | 1977 | | 1985 | | 1989 | | 1991 | |
|---|---|---|---|---|---|---|---|---|---|---|
| | Number | Percent | Number | Percent | Number | Percent | Number | Percent | Number | Percent |
| New England | 1,566 | 8.1 | 1,407 | 7.1 | 1,455 | 7.5 | 1,298 | 6.7 | 1,138 | 6.2 |
| Middle Atlantic | 4,325 | 22.3 | 3,569 | 18.4 | 3,095 | 16.1 | 2,876 | 14.8 | 2,593 | 14.1 |
| East north central | 5,115 | 26.3 | 4,967 | 25.1 | 4,221 | 21.9 | 4,285 | 22.0 | 4,077 | 22.1 |
| West north central | 1,226 | 6.3 | 1,327 | 6.7 | 1,316 | 6.8 | 1,403 | 7.2 | 1,380 | 7.5 |
| South Atlantic | 2,569 | 13.2 | 2,878 | 14.6 | 3,083 | 16.0 | 3,183 | 16.4 | 3,002 | 16.3 |
| East south central | 1,132 | 5.8 | 1,377 | 7.0 | 1,327 | 6.9 | 1,438 | 7.4 | 1,408 | 7.6 |
| West south central | 1,106 | 5.7 | 1,469 | 7.4 | 1,558 | 8.1 | 1,551 | 8.0 | 1,576 | 8.6 |
| Mountain | 322 | 1.7 | 477 | 2.4 | 612 | 3.2 | 644 | 3.3 | 629 | 3.4 |
| Pacific | 2,068 | 10.6 | 2,238 | 11.3 | 2,605 | 13.5 | 2,780 | 14.3 | 2,628 | 14.3 |
| U.S. total | 19,469 | 100.0 | 19,709 | 100.0 | 19,272 | 100.0 | 19,457 | 100.0 | 18,430 | 100.0 |

Source: Department of Labor, Bureau of Labor Statistics, Current Employment Statistics, State and Area Industry Employment data.

added had fallen to 50.5 percent, and in the next twenty years it plummeted to just 38.2 percent.[17] Moreover, the 1967–87 decline occurred in a period when national manufacturing ceased to grow.

The popular explanations for the recent declining fortunes of Rust Belt manufacturing are the sharp rise in oil prices in the 1970s, the rise in imports caused by the strong dollar in the early 1980s, and the shift of final demand away from heavy, metals-related industries on which the North had traditionally relied.[18] None of these explanations is persuasive for explaining the 1947–67 decline, of course, but if the first two are correct, one might have expected to see a rebound in Rust Belt manufacturing in the late 1980s or early 1990s because the real value of the dollar and real crude energy prices declined by more than one-third in 1985–88.[19]

As table 1-7 shows, however, there has been no rebound in Rust Belt manufacturing employment since 1985. Between 1985 and 1989, U.S. manufacturing employment grew infinitesimally—by about 160,000, or about 0.8 percent—but manufacturing employment in the middle Atlantic and east north central regions *declined* by about 150,000, or from 38 percent of the national total to 36 percent. In 1990–91, U.S. manufacturing was mired in a recession; by 1991 manufacturing employment had fallen by about 1 million. During this recession, manufacturing employment in the middle Atlantic region continued to decline more rapidly than the national trend, but in the east north central region it stabilized at about 22 percent of U.S. manufacturing jobs. Thus, seven years after the peak of the exchange rate and eleven years after the peak in energy prices, there has been no recovery in Rust Belt manufacturing employment.

Could this continued decline in the Rust Belt be due to the fact that these regions have a disproportionate share of industries that are exhibiting slow growth nationally? If so, one might conclude that many of this region's problems are not a reflection of its underlying comparative advantage as a manufacturing center but are

17. The Rust Belt share declined at a 1.4 percent annual rate between 1967 and 1987, but only at a 0.8 percent rate between 1947 and 1967. Bureau of the Census, *Census of Manufactures* (Department of Commerce, 1967, 1987).

18. See Branson and Love, "Real Exchange Rate and Employment."

19. Real exchange rate from Board of Governors, Federal Reserve System; producer price index for crude energy price (from Department of Labor, Bureau of Labor Statistics) deflated by the GDP implicit price deflator from Department of Commerce, Bureau of Economic Analysis.

Table 1-8. **Regional Manufacturing Employment Growth, Actual and Predicted, 1977–89**
Thousands

| Region | 1977 actual | 1985 actual | 1985 predicted[a] | Excess 1977–85 growth | 1989 actual | 1989 predicted[a] | Excess 1977–89 growth | Excess 1989–85 difference |
|---|---|---|---|---|---|---|---|---|
| New England | 1,407.2 | 1,455.4 | 1,391.3 | 64.1 | 1,297.6 | 1,390.7 | −93.1 | −157.2 |
| Middle Atlantic | 3,568.8 | 3,095.4 | 3,477.5 | −382.1 | 2,875.6 | 3,486.3 | −610.7 | −228.6 |
| East north central | 4,967.4 | 4,221.0 | 4,915.6 | −694.6 | 4,285.3 | 4,955.3 | −670.0 | 24.6 |
| West north central | 1,326.7 | 1,316.0 | 1,324.5 | −8.5 | 1,403.1 | 1,337.6 | 65.5 | 74.0 |
| South Atlantic | 2,878.2 | 3,082.6 | 2,698.9 | 383.7 | 3,183.0 | 2,733.8 | 449.2 | 65.5 |
| East south central | 1,376.8 | 1,327.4 | 1,309.0 | 18.4 | 1,457.9 | 1,314.7 | 123.2 | 104.8 |
| West south central | 1,469.3 | 1,558.2 | 1,431.9 | 126.3 | 1,550.8 | 1,455.6 | 115.2 | −11.1 |
| Mountain | 476.7 | 611.5 | 474.4 | 137.1 | 644.4 | 480.5 | 163.9 | 26.8 |
| Pacific | 2,238.0 | 2,605.0 | 2,245.0 | 360.0 | 2,779.6 | 2,279.2 | 500.4 | 140.4 |
| Rust Belt[b] | 8,536.2 | 7,316.4 | 8,393.1 | −1,076.7 | 7,160.9 | 8,441.6 | −1,280.7 | −204.0 |
| South[c] | 5,724.3 | 5,968.2 | 5,439.8 | 528.4 | 6,171.7 | 5,484.1 | 687.6 | 159.2 |
| West[d] | 2,714.7 | 3,216.5 | 2,719.4 | 497.1 | 3,424.0 | 2,759.7 | 664.3 | 167.2 |

Source: Department of Labor, BLS, Current Employment Statistics, State and Area Industry Employment data.
a. Based on growth in two-digit manufacturing industry employment for the entire country, using 1977 *Census of Manufactures* industry employment shares for each state as weights.
b. Middle Atlantic and east north central.
c. South Atlantic, east south central, and west south central.
d. Mountain and Pacific.

rather caused by larger global trends affecting certain industries that are heavily represented in the industrial Northeast.

## The Rust Belt since 1977

It is widely believed that Rust Belt manufacturing has declined since the 1970s because it is the home of several troubled industries, such as steel, machine tools, and motor vehicles. To test for the structural composition effect, I analyze changes in employment since 1977 for each region, constructing predictions for growth in employment based on the assumption that employment in each two-digit industry grew at the same rate in each state as in the United States as a whole.[20] Table 1-8 exhibits the results. Both Rust Belt regions performed less well than would be expected if they simply mirrored the national growth rates in each industry weighted by their 1977 regional industry employment shares. In the east north central and middle Atlantic regions, the manufacturing sector underperformed the national economy by more than 1 million jobs between 1977 and 1985, the year in which the value of the dollar peaked. Had these regions' industries shown the same employment growth between 1977 and 1985 as the entire country, they would have lost less than 150,000 jobs instead of the nearly 1.1 million jobs they did lose. Among the northern regions, only New England outperformed the entire economy in 1977–85. By 1989 the Rust Belt underperformance had reached nearly 1.3 million jobs.[21]

The fall in the dollar and in real energy prices since 1985 has not reversed the decline in manufacturing employment in New England or the middle Atlantic states, but the decline does appear to have been arrested in the east north central states. Between 1985 and 1989, before the 1990–91 recession, the New England and middle Atlantic states lost nearly 400,000 more jobs than would have been expected from their 1977 industrial structure (table 1-8). The east north central states appear to have roughly mirrored the national performance in their industries in 1985–89 as employment in these states' manufacturing industries rose by 64,000, or about 1.5 per-

20. The initial year, 1977, was chosen because it is the benchmark year (in which the *Census of Manufactures* is collected) that immediately precedes the 1980–85 appreciation of the dollar.

21. I use 1989 as the terminal year of the analysis because it is the last nonrecession year for which data are available.

**Table 1-9. Employment in Metal-related Industries, Selected Years, 1967–89**

Thousands unless otherwise indicated

| Region and year | Industry and SIC code | | | | | | Total |
|---|---|---|---|---|---|---|---|
| | Primary metals (33) | Fabricated metal products (34) | Machinery (35) | Electrical machinery (36) | Transport equipment (37) | Instruments[a] (38) | |
| *East north central* | | | | | | | |
| 1967 | 508.5 | 583.1 | 804.3 | 572.4 | 709.5 | 90.4 | 3,268.2 |
| 1977 | 475.4 | 572.3 | 773.7 | 487.9 | 743.4 | 102.2 | 3,154.9 |
| 1989 | 296.0 | 482.1 | 626.0 | 351.0 | 613.0 | 128.6 | 2,496.7 |
| Percent change, 1967–89 | −41.8 | −17.3 | −22.2 | −38.7 | −13.6 | 42.3 | −23.6 |
| *Middle Atlantic* | | | | | | | |
| 1967 | 353.0 | 280.9 | 396.8 | 466.8 | 221.2 | 177.5 | 1,896.2 |
| 1977 | 280.4 | 253.3 | 363.6 | 359.2 | 173.1 | 192.3 | 1,621.9 |
| 1989 | 134.1 | 202.0 | 292.2 | 257.9 | 135.6 | 227.1 | 1,248.9 |
| Percent change, 1967–89 | −62.0 | −28.1 | −26.4 | −44.8 | −28.7 | 27.9 | −34.1 |
| *U.S. total* | | | | | | | |
| 1967 | 1,267.0 | 1,556.1 | 1,991.1 | 1,614.6 | 2,058.4 | 801.1 | 9,288.3 |
| 1977 | 1,181.6 | 1,579.4 | 2,198.4 | 1,594.0 | 1,860.6 | 846.2 | 9,260.2 |
| 1989 | 772.0 | 1,445.9 | 2,131.9 | 1,753.4 | 2,054.4 | 1,025.5 | 9,183.1 |
| Percent change, 1967–89 | −39.1 | −7.1 | 7.1 | 8.6 | −0.2 | 28.0 | −1.1 |

Source: Department of Labor, BLS, Current Employment Statistics, State and Area Industry Employment data; and Bureau of the Census, *County Business Patterns, 1967, 1977* (Department of Commerce, 1968, 1979).

a. Included because changes in SIC industry codes in 1987 transferred some establishments from SIC 36 (electrical machinery or electronic equipment) to SIC 38 (instruments).

cent. More recent evidence from the 1990–91 recession also suggests no revival of Rust Belt manufacturing relative to the rest of the country (table 1-7). Thus manufacturing has not rebounded from its 1982–85 nadir in the Northeast, but it has at least stabilized in the Great Lakes states. The Pacific and east south central states have continued to attract employment more rapidly than predicted from national industry growth trends. Conversely, the New England and west south central states grew less rapidly during 1985–89 than would have been expected given their 1977 industrial composition.

### The Role of Metal-related Industries

It is perhaps surprising that the growth in the economy in the late 1980s, the fall in energy prices, and the depreciation in the dollar have not served to slow or stop the decline in Rust Belt manufacturing. A look at the employment trends by two-digit industry provides some insight into the absence of this turnaround. Between 1977 and 1985, employment in transportation equipment, instruments, and electrical machinery grew quite rapidly; machinery employment was virtually constant; and employment in primary metals and fabricated metal products fell rapidly. After 1985 employment in the transportation equipment industry continued to expand, but it fell in all the other metals-related businesses. Thus there was no stunning turnaround in employment in these heavy durable-goods industries in response to lower energy prices, a lower dollar, or recent macroeconomic events. The sharp improvements that did occur after 1985 were in such nondurable goods industries as chemicals, paper, textiles, and food products. Several of these industries are located predominantly in the South; none is overwhelmingly associated with the Rust Belt.

A closer look at the east north central and middle Atlantic states' true base—the metals-related industries—is quite revealing. These industries accounted for 63 percent and 44 percent of these regions' 1967 manufacturing employment, respectively. Between 1967 and 1989, total U.S. employment in these industries changed little; employment dropped by about 1 percent after 1977 after remaining roughly constant during 1967–77 (table 1-9). The east north central states lost nearly 800,000 jobs in these industries in this period, however, which was about 87 percent of their total loss of manufacturing employment. The middle Atlantic states lost another 650,000

**Table 1-10. Excess Employment Growth within Two-Digit Industries, 1977–87[a]**

| Industry | New England | Middle Atlantic | East north central | West north central | South | West |
|---|---|---|---|---|---|---|
| Primary metals (33) | −4,485 | −35,935 | 6,447 | 4,117 | 23,817 | 5,959 |
| Fabricated metal products (34) | −7,587 | −19,894 | −44,388 | 19,632 | 24,465 | 24,755 |
| Machinery (35) | −11,702 | −56,940 | −63,739 | 6,737 | 59,547 | 66,101 |
| Electrical machinery (36) | 16,232 | −61,171 | −118,260 | −20,909 | 61,830 | 122,292 |
| Transport equipment (37) | 8,329 | −51,774 | −34,689 | 17,075 | 75,600 | −14,544 |
| Total for five industries | | | | | | |
| Excess | 787 | −225,714 | −254,629 | 26,652 | 245,259 | 204,563 |
| Actual | 39,803 | −322,460 | −653,770 | 11,332 | 161,126 | 377,399 |

Source: Department of the Census, *County Business Patterns, 1977.*

a. Estimates based on average employment growth in three-digit industries within each two-digit industry.

jobs in these industries, nearly 50 percent of their loss in manufacturing employment. Had these two regions held their share of employment in just these five two-digit industries—that is, had they matched the U.S. trend in these industries—they would have lost only about 850,000 manufacturing jobs from 1967 through 1989, not the 2.3 million total they did lose. In short, nearly two-thirds of the region's manufacturing problems may be traced to a loss of jobs in these five industries to other parts of the United States.

It is possible that even these job losses in the metals-related industries are due to intra-industry demand shifts. For instance, growth in aircraft manufacturing may have offset declining automobile industry demand. This would have increased employment in Washington, California, and Texas at the expense of Michigan, Ohio, Illinois, and Indiana. Thus it is necessary to examine shifts in three- or four-digit industry groups to determine whether the Rust Belt has suffered a decline in relative advantage.

Unfortunately, complete three- or four-digit employment data are not available by state from the Bureau of Labor Statistics (BLS) or the Census Bureau for recent years. The most recent data are the County Business Pattern data for establishments by county and by three-digit industry. Analyzing the relative shifts in these data for the various census regions over 1977–87 leads to the same conclusion: the middle Atlantic and east north central states have lost far more jobs in these five industries than the national growth trends for the three-digit industries in each would predict. The middle Atlantic states lost 322,460 jobs in these industries over the decade— 225,714 more than would have been predicted by a model of uniform national growth in the three-digit industry subcategories (table 1-10). The east north central states lost 254,629 more than predicted. Thus slightly more than half the job losses in these industries in these two regions must be attributed to factors other than shifting intra-industry demand patterns.

### The Impact of Foreign Trade

If the deteriorating U.S. trade balance in the early to mid-1980s is to blame for the decline in Rust Belt manufacturing, one should expect to see this effect in the industries most affected by trade. To test for such an effect, I analyzed the changes in regional employment since 1967 by two-digit manufacturing industry. The percentage change in each industry's employment was regressed on that industry's national ratio of exports to domestic shipments and its ratio of imports to apparent domestic supply in 1977. In each of the coastal regions, except for the middle Atlantic states, changes in employment were more strongly related to the export ratio than to the import ratio. (There was no relationship between employment growth and *the rate of change* in the export or import ratio.) Exports were directly and significantly associated with employment growth in every coastal region except the middle Atlantic in 1977–89, but import penetration was statistically significant with the expected negative sign only in the south Atlantic states.

In the middle Atlantic states, the trade variables explain virtually none of the variance in manufacturing employment growth despite the sharp decline in employment in this region after 1967. The pattern of decline in this region is simply not the same as the pattern of U.S. trade. Similarly, in the remaining "interior" regions, there is no relationship between the level or rate of change of the trade variables and the pattern of manufacturing employment growth.

A recent set of papers by William Branson and James Love conclude that the sharp rise in the dollar between 1980 and 1985 reduced U.S. manufacturing employment by about 5.5 percent.[22] Their results show that the largest effects of the dollar were in the central census regions. They find little effect of the dollar's appreciation in the New England and middle Atlantic regions' manufacturing sectors.

The Branson and Love results are obtained from a loglinear regression analysis of manufacturing employment on the real value of the dollar, real consumer energy prices, the national unemployment rate, and a time trend for 1970–86.[23] I have attempted to replicate their results with annual data from 1967 through 1990, lagging real energy and exchange rate variables by one year but using the contemporaneous unemployment rate. My results are similar to Bran-

22. See Branson and Love, "Real Exchange Rate and Employment," for a detailed bibliography.
23. Their model is estimated with quarterly data. The real exchange rate is the International Monetary Fund's index of relative labor costs in the United States. Real energy prices are measured by the ratio of the energy component of the consumer price index for urban workers to the overall CPI. The unemployment rate is the BLS measure for the entire United States. All independent variables enter with the current value and lagged values for each of the previous four quarters.

**Table 1-11. Coefficients of Exchange Rate Variable in Manufacturing Employment Regressions**[a]

| Region | 1968–80 (Crandall, annual data) | 1968–85 (Crandall, annual data) | 1968–90 (Crandall, annual data) | 1970:I–1986:I (Branson-Love, quarterly data) |
|---|---|---|---|---|
| New England | 0.02 | − 0.09* | − 0.05 | − 0.02 |
| Middle Atlantic | 0.06 | − 0.11* | − 0.07 | − 0.06* |
| East north central | − 0.06 | − 0.26* | − 0.04 | − 0.31* |
| West north central | − 0.16* | − 0.24* | − 0.10 | − 0.24* |
| South Atlantic | 0.03 | − 0.11* | − 0.03 | − 0.06* |
| East south central | − 0.07 | − 0.23* | − 0.05 | − 0.23* |
| West south central | − 0.05 | − 0.35* | − 0.19* | − 0.34* |
| Mountain | 0.02 | − 0.22* | − 0.04 | − 0.17* |
| Pacific | − 0.11 | − 0.18* | − 0.11* | − 0.15* |

*Statistically significant at 95 percent confidence level.

a. Equation estimated: log manufacturing employment = $a_0$ + $a_1$ TIME + $a_2$ log real exchange rate$_{t-1}$ + $a_3$ log real U.S. energy price$_{t-1}$ + $a_4$ log U.S. unemployment rate$_t$. Coefficient estimates reported above are for $a_2$. First-order serial correlation corrected by Cochran-Orcutt method.

son and Love's for 1968–85, but very different for 1968–80 and 1968–90 (see table 1-11).

The coefficients of the exchange rate variable for each of the three time periods, along with Branson and Love's 1970–86 results, are shown for each of the nine census regions in table 1-11. Note that the coefficients are almost evenly distributed between positive and negative values in 1968–80. Once 1981–85 is included, however, the coefficients become uniformly negative and highly statistically significant. When 1986–90 is added, the coefficients move once again toward zero, and only two are statistically significant.[24] Since the real value of the dollar generally fell during 1968–85, it is possible that the effects of the exchange rate are highly asymmetrical, or, alternatively, that the rise in the dollar simply accelerated the adjustment that was already under way for other reasons.

The Branson and Love results suggest that the exchange rate had very little effect on manufacturing in the middle Atlantic states in 1981–86 but a very large effect in the east north central states. Yet manufacturing employment in the east north central states fell from 26.1 percent to 23 percent of the U.S. total between 1970 and 1980, while the decline was only to 21.9 percent in the next five years.

24. When the 1968–85 regression estimates are used to forecast 1989 employment, they overpredict by 10 to 20 percent in the three Rust Belt regions. Thus the decline in the real value of the dollar and in energy prices has not rekindled manufacturing employment growth according to the estimated 1968–80 relationship.

Since 1986 this share has stabilized at 22 percent. Ironically, the middle Atlantic states' share of total manufacturing employment has continued to decline since 1980 at the same rate as during 1967–80.

Thus any attempt to link the long-run decline of Rust Belt manufacturing employment to the value of the dollar is difficult to defend because this decline has persisted through periods of dollar appreciation and depreciation. Even Branson and Love's results do not point to a general effect on the Rust Belt, but they do attribute more than 80 percent of the decline in the east north central region's manufacturing employment in 1980–85 to the rise in the value of the dollar.

Nonetheless, the results in table 1-11 are consistent with the theory that the 1980–85 appreciation of the dollar contributed to the problems experienced by U.S. manufacturing in the central United States, including the Great Lakes states. Moreover, they suggest that the effects of currency fluctuations on manufacturing are not symmetrical. The 1986–90 depreciation of the dollar has not generated a rebound in manufacturing employment in these same central regions. These results are thus consistent with the modern economic theory of "hysteresis"—the tendency of investment or exit decisions to be delayed in response to changes in underlying conditions in an uncertain environment. Under this theory, the decline in some regions and their failure to recover throughout the 1980s may be attributed to the rise in the dollar that reduced the option value of keeping uneconomic plants open and the failure of the recent dollar depreciation to move firms to the point of exercising their options to build new ones.[25]

However one interprets the data from the 1980s, any analysis of the Rust Belt's loss of manufacturing must come to grips with the fact that it began many decades earlier. In fact, manufacturing employment in both Rust Belt regions was very close to its longer-term trend once again in 1990, given the rate of change in total U.S. manufacturing employment.[26] The only regions far below trends in

25. See Avinash Dixit, "Investment and Hysteresis," *Journal of Economic Perspectives*, vol. 6 (Winter 1992), pp. 107–32. An analysis of plant closings, openings, expansions, and contractions is provided in the next chapter.

26. Predictions of 1980–90 manufacturing employment for each region were obtained from a regression of the logarithm of the region's manufacturing employment

manufacturing employment by 1990 were the mountain and south central regions, undoubtedly because of the collapse of the energy boom. In the next chapter, I shall examine the causes of manufacturing's exodus from the Rust Belt over the past quarter century, not simply the recent movements in manufacturing among regions.

## Other Sectors

In 1967 the two Rust Belt census regions accounted for 56 percent of gross U.S. manufacturing output. By 1989—before the recent recession—their share of manufacturing output had fallen to 38 percent. By contrast, in this same twenty-two-year period, the decline in the Rust Belt's share of all U.S. gross output was only from 40 percent to 33 percent.[27] Thus the Rust Belt's relative decline in manufacturing was about double its decline in total output.

Given these trends, it is clear that economic resources in the Rust Belt have not simply fled to the South and West, but rather that they have also shifted to other sectors within the Rust Belt. In particular, Rust Belt labor has been diverted from manufacturing to a variety of other sectors, often resulting in lower wages. Between 1977 and 1991 (the most recent complete year for which data are available), the Rust Belt states lost 1.6 million manufacturing jobs but gained 6.3 million nonmanufacturing, nonagricultural jobs. The effects of these employment shifts on the real incomes of those generally low- and medium-skilled workers displaced from manufacturing depend on the industries in which employment has been growing.

Between 1977 and 1985, employment in every sector grew less rapidly in the Rust Belt than in the United States as a whole (table 1-12). Manufacturing and mining were major underperformers in the Rust Belt during this period. After 1985 manufacturing and mining continued to lag behind the rest of the country, but some of this shortfall was offset by substantial growth in construction, finance, and services. Unfortunately, the real estate and construction boom that fed much of this growth in the mid- to late 1980s has

---

on time and the logarithm of national manufacturing employment between 1967 and 1979. By 1990, the middle Atlantic states were 2.2 percent above trend and the east north central states were 4.2 percent below trend.

27. Data from Department of Commerce, Bureau of Economic Analysis.

**Table 1-12.  U.S. and Rust Belt Nonfarm Employment Growth Rates, Selected Periods, 1977–91**

Percent

| Sector | 1977–85 | | 1985–91 | |
|---|---|---|---|---|
| | U.S. | Rust Belt[a] | U.S. | Rust Belt[a] |
| Total nonfarm | 2.1 | 0.9 | 1.7 | 1.2 |
| Manufacturing | − 0.3 | − 1.9 | − 0.7 | − 1.5 |
| Mining | 1.5 | − 1.8 | − 4.8 | − 5.5 |
| Construction | 2.4 | 1.1 | − 0.1 | 1.4 |
| Services | 4.5 | 3.7 | 4.1 | 3.3 |
| Finance | 3.6 | 2.7 | 1.8 | 1.8 |
| Transportation/ utilities | 1.4 | 0.1 | 1.6 | 1.0 |
| Retail/wholesale | 2.7 | 1.6 | 1.6 | 1.2 |
| Government | | | | |
| Total nonfarm less manufacturing | 2.7 | 1.8 | 2.3 | 1.9 |

Source: Department of Labor, BLS, Current Employment Statistics, State and Area Industry Employment data.

a. Middle Atlantic and east north central states.

now ended. Since 1989 construction employment has declined by more than 150,000 in these regions and financial employment has stopped growing. Thus the decline in manufacturing is no longer being cushioned by a surge in real estate, banking, and construction. The most rapidly growing sector in the Rust Belt—as in the United States as a whole—is the service sector. In chapter 3, I examine the possible effects of this structural shift on earned incomes. In the next chapter, I turn to the question of why manufacturing continues to move away from the Rust Belt.

*Chapter Two*

# Explaining the Regional Shift
# in Manufacturing

GIVEN THE ABUNDANCE of state, metropolitan area, and even establishment-specific data, the empirical literature on regional economic development has grown rapidly in the past decade. This literature—and new extensions of it—may be used to identify the causes of the Rust Belt's industrial decline.

There are two major strands to the applied economic literature on regional economic development. One begins with a neoclassical equilibrium model of a closed economy in which population growth, the savings rate, and technology combine to generate a convergence toward an equilibrium output per person. When the model is applied to an open economy, such as that in the United States, the rate of convergence is more rapid because of labor migration and capital mobility, but the persistence of differential rental rates on human capital suggests that neither capital nor labor is perfectly mobile.[1] As with the more traditional, ad hoc models of regional growth, the neoclassical approach allows for exogenous shocks that prevent full convergence to a common rate of output per unit of labor.

The other strand, the more traditional literature, uses a disequilibrium model to relate changes in regional output or employment to input prices, taxes, government expenditures on human capital or infrastructure, and the general environment, generally in an open economy.[2] Capital and employment (and thus output) move from less attractive (higher costs, poorer climate) to more attractive areas.

1. See Robert J. Barro and Xavier Sala-i-Martin, "Economic Growth and Convergence across the United States," Working Paper 3419 (Cambridge, Mass.: National Bureau of Economic Research, August 1990), for a discussion of the application of the neoclassical growth model to open and closed economies.

2. See, for example, Leonard F. Wheat, *Regional Growth and Industrial Location: An Empirical Viewpoint* (Lexington, Mass.: Lexington Books, 1973).

The migration of capital and labor tends to narrow interregional differences, but exogenous demand and supply shocks prevent the attainment of full equilibrium.

## Convergence?

In recent work, Robert Barro and Xavier Sala-i-Martin estimate the rate of convergence of per capita income and output across the United States, using data on personal income and gross state product produced by the Department of Commerce.[3] In one variant, they estimate the following equation for the growth in total gross state product per person and for its components, such as manufacturing, mining, construction, and trade.

$$(2\text{-}1) \qquad \log(y_t/y_{t-1}) / T = a + [(1 - e^{-\beta T})/T] \log y_{t-1},$$

where $\beta$ is the estimated annual rate of convergence in $y$, the output per person or output per worker, and $T$ is the length of the time period between $t - 1$ and $t$. They find that the estimated rate of convergence for 1963–86 is highest for manufacturing. However, they do not explore the determinants of convergence across sectors, nor do they relate the convergence in output per worker to regional wage differentials or other influences.

Barro and Sala-i-Martin point out that convergence can be measured in two ways: the rate at which the dispersion in output per person declines over time—a phenomenon that I refer to as "overall" convergence—and the "systematic" rate at which endogenous forces reduce preexisting differences in output per person—or $\beta$ in equation 2-1. Because of supply and demand shocks, there may be no overall convergence despite a substantial general tendency of factor supply flows, savings shifts, and technological forces to reduce differences in output per person over time.

The rate of *overall* convergence in manufacturing output per worker since 1967 may be measured by the changes in the standard deviation of its logarithm (table 2-1), using Department of Commerce data on gross state product (GSP) in manufacturing and state

3. Robert J. Barro and Xavier Sala-i-Martin, "Convergence across States and Regions," *Brookings Papers on Economic Activity, 1:1991*, pp. 107–58.

**Table 2-1. Dispersion of Gross State Manufacturing Product per Worker and Manufacturing Wages across States, Selected Years, 1967–89[a]**

| Year | Gross output per worker | Average manufacturing wage | Gross output per dollar of wages |
|------|------------------------|----------------------------|----------------------------------|
| 1967 | 0.194 | 0.146 | 0.150 |
| 1977 | 0.187 | 0.150 | 0.131 |
| 1989 | 0.130 | 0.117 | 0.115 |

Sources: Department of Labor, Bureau of Labor Statistics, Current Employment Statistics, State and Area Industry Employment data; and data from Department of Commerce, Bureau of Economic Analysis, Regional Economic Analysis Division.
a. Standard deviation of the natural logarithm. Excludes District of Columbia, Alaska, and Hawaii.

**Table 2-2. Estimated Rate of Systematic Convergence ($\beta$) in Manufacturing Gross State Product per Worker, Selected Periods, 1967–89[a]**

| Period | Without regional dummies | With regional dummies |
|--------|--------------------------|-----------------------|
| 1967–77 | 0.028 | 0.028 |
| 1977–89 | 0.036 | 0.033 |
| 1967–89 | 0.024 | 0.024 |

Source: Ordinary least squares estimates of $\beta$ in equation 2-1, using Department of Commerce data on GSP and Department of Labor data on manufacturing employment.
a. Excludes District of Columbia, Alaska, and Hawaii.

employment data from the Bureau of Labor Statistics. These data show little overall convergence across the forty-eight mainland states in the decade from 1967 to 1977 but a rapid convergence thereafter. Thus the gap in output per worker (average labor productivity) across states appears to have been reduced at an increasing rate in the twenty-two years after 1967, but this narrowing could have occurred without any shift of manufacturing from the Rust Belt to the South and West.

Nor does the overall convergence necessarily reflect a similar reduction in the variance in unit labor costs across states. During this same period, manufacturing wage rates were converging more modestly (table 2-1). As a result, the convergence in output per worker per dollar of wages—the reciprocal of unit labor costs—has been much slower than the convergence in productivity.

I have also estimated the degree to which *systematic* convergence has been occurring across states by estimating equation 2-1 for manufacturing GSP. The results for 1967–89 generally confirm the pattern for general convergence (table 2-2). As with overall conver-

**Table 2-3. Manufacturing Gross State Product per Worker, Selected Years, 1967–89[a]**

Thousands of 1982 dollars

| Region | 1967 | 1977 | 1989 |
|--------|------|------|------|
| New England | 21.86 | 28.10 | 49.07 |
| Middle Atlantic | 24.97 | 32.71 | 47.94 |
| East north central | 28.37 | 38.33 | 49.99 |
| West north central | 24.28 | 33.42 | 48.91 |
| South Atlantic | 20.53 | 28.24 | 38.47 |
| East south central | 22.50 | 29.82 | 41.41 |
| West south central | 28.95 | 39.49 | 56.92 |
| Mountain | 26.65 | 32.06 | 45.31 |
| Pacific | 27.90 | 34.70 | 52.51 |
| U.S. average | 25.44 | 33.71 | 47.78 |

Source: Department of Labor, BLS, Current Employment Statistics, State and Area Industry Employment data; and data from Department of Commerce, BEA, Regional Economic Analysis Division.
a. Excludes District of Columbia, Alaska, and Hawaii.

gence, the rate of systematic convergence accelerated markedly between 1967–77 and 1977– 89.[4]

These results allow one to conclude that there has been a considerable narrowing in the dispersion across states of average productivity in manufacturing since 1967 and that this convergence process accelerated after 1977. But this convergence has not resulted in an equally dramatic reduction in the dispersion in the ratio of productivity to average manufacturing wages. Moreover, this evidence tells little about the *causes* of the recent convergence in manufacturing productivity. It is consistent with a wide range of possible patterns of labor migration or migration of industry.

The lack of any simple relationship between the convergence in productivity and the regional shift in manufacturing is evident when one examines the regional distribution of GSP per worker in manufacturing in 1967, 1977, and 1989 (table 2-3). Manufacturing activity shifted from the North to the southern regions between 1967 and 1977; thereafter, the shift continued to the South but even more strongly to the West. Yet between 1967 and 1977 there was little apparent change in the gap in manufacturing GSP per worker between the northern and southern regions. In the rapidly growing south Atlantic region, for example, GSP per worker remained about

4. The results are reported with and without a set of eight census regional dummies simply because Barro and Sala-i-Martin employed a set of dummy variables in their empirical investigation. Note that the results are not much affected by the inclusion of these dummies.

17 percent below the national average. In 1967 the Pacific region enjoyed manufacturing GSP per worker that was 10 percent above the national average; this was still true twenty-two years later, after enormous growth in its manufacturing sector.

The northeastern region exhibits a rather surprising pattern. Between 1967 and 1989, New England's manufacturing GSP per worker rose from 14 percent below the national average to 3 percent above average even though its share of manufacturing remained relatively constant. At the same time, the east north central states' GSP per worker declined relative to the national average by 6 percentage points, while in the middle Atlantic region—where manufacturing fell the most dramatically—GSP per manufacturing worker actually rose relative to the national average.

Because convergence in productivity is consistent with a variety of regional trends in migration, capital-labor ratios, and industrial growth, there is little to be learned about the relative determinants of regional growth in manufacturing from looking further at the convergence in incomes or productivity levels. It is necessary to look more directly at the growth in manufacturing output, employment, and capital.

## Explaining the Migration of Industry

Whatever the evidence on convergence across regions or states, the geographic migration of manufacturing is indisputable. The fact that this migration continues decade after decade calls for an explanation. Why do the northern states—particularly those in the Rust Belt—continue to lose manufacturing jobs? Why has an equilibrium not been reached after decades of this migration?

### Previous Studies

There is a sizable literature on the determinants of regional economic growth. Most of these studies focus on the growth in total employment or manufacturing employment, using single-equation regression techniques to relate a variety of regional variables at the beginning of the period to the rate of change over the period. These "reduced-form" estimates combine the effects of population migration with those caused by changing business location, thereby making it difficult to determine if jobs are chasing population or vice versa. Richard Muth recognized this problem in the 1970s, and Michael Greenwood elaborated on it in his research and his survey of the subject.[5] While the reduced-form equations may be useful in predicting future growth, they may not be able to disentangle the forces affecting migration and population growth from those affecting the regional distribution of industrial activity. Nevertheless, even recent work typically relies on single-equation regression analysis.[6]

The literature on the determinants of business location has grown considerably in recent years. The focus of these studies varies substantially: business formations, new plant start-ups, direct foreign investment, employment growth in particular industries, manufacturing employment, nonfarm employment, personal income, and gross state product.[7] The explanatory variables typically included in such studies are generally measures of taxes, tax incentives, public expenditures, wage rates, and the degree of unionization.

Earlier studies often yielded inconclusive results on the effects of taxes and government expenditures on business activity, but recent studies tend to find that growth is inversely related to taxes. Timothy Bartik's review of these studies shows that the elasticity of growth with respect to taxes is relatively small for interstate or intermetropolitan area studies but much greater for intrastate or intra-area studies.[8] The effects of state and local government expenditure policies are generally less robust. Most find some effects for one or more measures of spending—welfare, transportation, education, police and fire—but many other categories of spending have insignificant effects. The results for labor market variables in this litera-

5. Richard F. Muth, "Migration: Chicken or Egg?" *Southern Economic Journal*, vol. 37 (January 1971), pp. 295–305; and Michael J. Greenwood, "Research on Internal Migration in the United States: A Survey," *Journal of Economic Literature*, vol. 13 (June 1975), pp. 397–433.

6. See, for example, Alicia H. Munnell, "How Does Public Infrastructure Affect Regional Economic Performance?" *New England Economic Review* (September–October 1990), pp. 11–32.

7. For a useful summary of this literature, see John P. Blair and Robert Premus, "Major Features in Industrial Location: A Review," *Economic Development Quarterly*, vol. 1 (February 1987), pp. 72–85; and Timothy J. Bartik, *Who Benefits from State and Local Economic Development Policies?* (Kalamazoo: W. E. Upjohn Institute for Employment Research, 1991), pp. 17–62.

8. Bartik, *Who Benefits*.

ture are somewhat uneven. Most studies find that business growth is inversely related to wage rates or unionization, but the collinearity of wages with unionization makes the identification of these effects difficult.

While much of the existing literature provides useful insights for explaining the pattern of industrial growth, a substantial share of it applies to either a much narrower or much broader domain than the focus of this book: the regional distribution of U.S. manufacturing employment and output. Moreover, few of these studies cover a long period of recent history. In the remainder of this chapter, therefore, I focus on the regional distribution of U.S. manufacturing over the past quarter century.

### New Empirical Estimates

To model the growth in a region's manufacturing employment or output, it is crucial to understand that such growth is the net result of the opening of new plants, expansions or contractions by existing plants, and the closure of obsolete plants. The effect of various microeconomic variables on each of these phenomena may differ substantially. For instance, state taxes may affect a firm's choice of a location for a new plant, but they may be much less important in the decision to expand or contract an existing plant. Similarly, the degree of unionization in a state or metropolitan area may affect the location decision for a new plant, but strong unions may make it very difficult for a firm to phase down or close a plant.[9] Because many cross-sectional studies of regional economic growth attempt to explain the net result of all of these expansion and contraction decisions, they may fail to uncover significant causal relationships in the migration of business activity.

I begin with a standard disequilibrium model of regional employment (or output) growth:

$$(2\text{-}2) \quad EMP_{it} = EMP_{i,t-1} + \lambda \, (EMP^*_{it} - EMP_{i,\,t-1}) \; 0 < \lambda < 1,$$

where $EMP_{it}$ is employment in the $i$th state (or area) in year $t$, $EMP^*_{it}$ is equilibrium employment in the $i$th region in year $t$, and $\lambda$

9. For instance, the United Steelworkers have negotiated very expensive early-retirement provisions in major steel company contracts, substantially reducing these firms' ability to close obsolete plants.

is the annual rate of adjustment to equilibrium. $EMP_{it}^*$ is, in turn, a function of the initial employment level $EMP_{i,t-\tau}$ and those micro-economic or environmental variables that affect producers' and labor's location decisions:

$$(2\text{-}3) \qquad\qquad EMP_{it}^* = \alpha\, EMP_{i,t-\tau}^{\beta}\, e^{f(\ )\tau u_i}.$$

The term $e^{f(\ )\tau}$ is the exponential growth rate, $f(\ )$ contains the relevant microeconomic and environmental variables, and $u_i$ is a random-error term.

Substituting equation 2-3 into 2-2 and lagging $EMP_i$ by $\tau$ years yields

$$(2\text{-}4) \quad EMP_{it} - \{1 - \lambda - \lambda(1-\lambda) - \lambda[1 - \lambda - \lambda(1-\lambda)] - ...\}\, EMP_{i,t-\tau}$$
$$= \{\lambda + \lambda(1-\lambda) + \lambda\,[1 - \lambda - \lambda(1-\lambda)]...\}\, \alpha\, EMP_{i,t-\tau}^{\beta}\, e^{f(\ )\tau u_i}.$$

As $\tau$ becomes large, the left-hand side of equation 2-4 approaches $EMP_{it}$ and the adjustment factor on the right-hand side approaches unity, and the equation may be written simply as

$$(2\text{-}4\text{a}) \qquad\qquad EMP_{it} = \alpha\, EMP_{i,t-\tau}^{\beta}\, e^{f(\ )\tau u_i}.$$

To estimate equation 2-4a, I simply divide both sides by $EMP_{i,t-\tau}$ and take natural logarithms of both sides:

$$(2\text{-}5) \quad \log\!\left(\frac{EMP_{it}}{EMP_{i,t-\tau}}\right) = \log \alpha + (\beta - 1) \log EMP_{i,t-\tau} + f(\ )\tau + u_i.$$

If there are no economies or diseconomies from agglomeration, $\beta$ should be equal to 1 and equation 2-5 simply becomes

$$(2\text{-}6) \qquad\qquad \log\!\left(\frac{EMP_{it}}{EMP_{i,t-\tau}}\right) = \log \alpha + f(\ )\tau + u_i.$$

A priori reasoning and previous research suggest that input prices, unionization, state tax rates, state government expenditures, state infrastructure, and local climate enter the expression $f(\ )$. When these independent variables are introduced into $f(\ )$, equation 2-6 takes the final form,

$$(2\text{-}6\text{a}) \quad \log\,(EMP_{it}/EMP_{i,t-\tau}) = \log \alpha_0 + \alpha_1\tau WAGE_{i,t-\tau}$$
$$+ \alpha_2\tau UNION_{i,t-\tau} + \alpha_3\tau P_{i,t-\tau} + TAX_{i,t-\tau} + \alpha_5\tau DEMAND_{i,t-\tau}$$
$$+ \alpha_6\tau GOVT_{i,t-\tau} + \alpha_7\tau INFRA_{i,t-\tau} + \alpha_8\tau TEMP_{i,t-\tau} + u_i.$$

Thus the standard disequilibrium model is recast into an equilibrium model by utilizing long lags in the prospective empirical analysis. The coefficient of each structural variable increases with the lag ($\tau$) utilized.

*DEMAND* is a measure of the strength of demand in the region, *TAX* is a measure of taxes specific to the region, *WAGE* is the region's average wage rate, *GOVT* is a measure of the region's government spending on such things as education and welfare, *UNION* is a measure of the pervasiveness of unions in the region, *P* is a vector of other input costs such as energy, *INFRA* is a measure of the region's public infrastructure, and *TEMP* is some measure of the attractiveness of the region's climate.

To estimate equation 2-6, I use data from individual states and metropolitan areas. The period of analysis is 1967–89, and results are shown for 1967–77 and 1977–89. The choice of these years is based on the fact that 1967 and 1977 were years of the quinquennial *Census of Manufactures* and were both years of relatively strong macroeconomic performance. The terminal year, 1989, is the most recent nonrecession year. In some instances, 1987 is the terminal year because it is the year of the most recent *Census of Manufactures*.[10] Figure 2-1 demonstrates that the decline in manufacturing over the 1963–89 period in the Rust Belt regions has been continuous. Therefore the results reported below are not due to an arbitrary choice of time period.

### State Data

I begin the empirical analysis with data drawn from all fifty states and the District of Columbia.[11] A complete description of all variables and data sources appears in table 2-4. The dependent variable is the difference in the logarithms of either employment or gross state product. The wage variable is the residual from a standard human-capital equation estimated from the Current Population Survey data for 1967 and 1977. Many tax variables are available, but the one reported is the Advisory Commission on Intergovernmental Relations' (ACIR) estimate of state and local tax effort with respect to corporate taxes.[12] Unionization is measured by

10. I use 1991 as the terminal year in some estimates below simply to check the robustness of the results.

11. Because some data are unavailable for the District of Columbia, Alaska, and Hawaii, most results are reported for only forty-eight states.

12. Alternative measures of taxation are addressed below.

**Figure 2-1. Regional Share of Manufacturing Gross State Product and Employment, 1963-89**

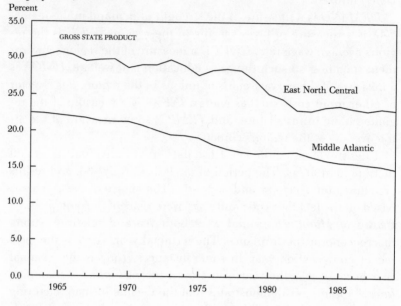

Percent

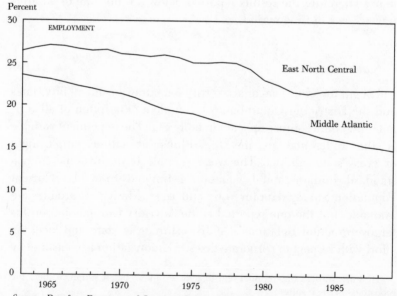

Percent

Sources:  Data from Department of Commerce, Bureau of Economic Analysis, Regional Economic Analysis Division (November 1991); and Department of Labor, Bureau of Labor Statistics, Current Employment Statistics, State and Area Industry Employment data.

## Table 2-4. Data Used in State Regressions

| Variable | Description | Source |
|---|---|---|
| EMP | Employment—nonfarm or manufacturing | Bureau of Labor Statistics[a] |
| GSP | Gross state product—nonfarm or manufacturing | Bureau of Economic Analysis[b] |
| WAGE | Annual earnings per worker, adjusted for age, sex, race, and experience | Current Population Survey[c] |
| UNION | Proportion of nonfarm workers in unions | Bureau of Labor Statistics, Grant Thornton[d] |
| TAX | Proportion of corporate tax capacity taxed by state | Advisory Commission on Intergovernmental Relations, National Institute of Education[e] |
| ENERGY | Cost per Btu of energy for industrial users | Department of Energy[f] |
| ZONE | Variable reflecting distance from manufacturing belt in 11 discrete zones | Leonard Wheat[g] |
| MARKET | Strength of demand, defined as total GSP divided by manufacturing GSP, multiplied by ZONE | Bureau of Economic Analysis[b] |
| MOUNTAIN REGION | Dummy variable for census mountain region | . . . |
| NORTHTIER | Dummy variable for Montana, North Dakota, Wyoming, Idaho | . . . |
| GOVT | Total state and local government spending per capita | Census of Governments[h] |
| INFRA | Real infrastructure stock per capita | Alicia Munnell[i] |
| TEMP | Mean January temperature | Census Bureau[j] |

a. Department of Labor, Bureau of Labor Statistics, Current Employment Statistics, State and Area Industry Employment data.

b. Data from Department of Commerce, Bureau of Economic Analysis, Regional Economic Analysis Division.

c. Current Population Survey (March 1968, 1978, 1990), machine-readable data file (Bureau of the Census, 1968, 1978, 1990).

d. Department of Labor, Bureau of Labor Statistics, *Directory of National and International Labor Unions in the United States, 1969*, bulletin 1665 (1970), p. 76; Department of Labor, Bureau of Labor Statistics, *Handbook of Labor Statistics*, bulletin 2070 (December 1980); *10th Annual Grant Thornton Manufacturing Climates Study* (Chicago: Grant Thornton, June 1989); and *11th Annual Grant Thornton Manufacturing Climates Study* (Chicago: Grant Thornton, August 1990).

e. Advisory Commission on Intergovernmental Relations, *Measuring the Fiscal Capacity and Effort of State and Local Areas* (March 1971), table G-5; and Department of Health, Education and Welfare, National Institute of Education, *Tax Wealth in Fifty States: 1977 Supplement* (October 1979), table 3.

f. Data from Department of Energy, Energy Information Administration, State Energy Price and Expenditure Data System, 1989.

g. Leonard F. Wheat, "The Determinants of 1963–77 Regional Manufacturing Growth: Why the South and West Grow," *Journal of Regional Science*, vol. 26 (November 1986), pp. 635–59.

h. Bureau of the Census, *1982 Census of Governments*, vol. 6, no. 4: "Historical Statistics on Governmental Finances and Employment" (Department of Commerce, January 1985), table 24.

i. Alicia H. Munnell, "How Does Public Infrastructure Affect Regional Economic Performance?" *New England Economic Review* (September–October 1990), pp. 11–32.

j. Bureau of the Census, *Statistical Abstract of the United States: 1990*, 110th ed. (Department of Commerce, 1990), table 364, p. 209.

union membership as a share of nonfarm employment as reported by the Bureau of Labor Statistics. Because data on the marginal cost of industrial land is unavailable, the only other general input-cost variable used in this analysis is *ENERGY*, the average price of energy to industrial users in each state.

The "demand" variables merit special comment. Leonard Wheat argues that manufacturing has shifted from the traditional northern manufacturing regions to the South and West in response to the growth of purchasing power relative to the supply of manufactures in the southern and western regions.[13] The effect of this increase in demand on manufacturing is related to the distance of the state from the traditional manufacturing regions because of transportation costs. Therefore, distance and demand interact in a variable called *MARKET*, which is equal to the ratio of total economic activity (or purchasing power) to manufacturing output multiplied by *ZONE*. *ZONE* is a measure of the distance from the traditional manufacturing belt. It assumes 11 integral values, with 1 being the northern manufacturing regions and 11 being the most distant states, Hawaii and Alaska.

Infrastructure (*INFRA*) variables supplied by Alicia Munnell of the Federal Reserve Bank of Boston include the real capital stock invested in water and sewer facilities, highways, and all other infrastructure, divided by the state's population.[14] State and local current spending per capita is available from the *Census of Governments*. Two other dummy variables are used in the analysis, one for the mountain region and one for Montana, North Dakota, Idaho, and Wyoming (*NORTHTIER*). The mountain region has systematically outperformed the rest of the country in manufacturing growth even after accounting for the microeconomic variables in my analysis. *NORTHTIER* is inserted to capture the effects of the hostile environment for building infrastructure, such as highways, for modern commerce in these four northern states.

13. Wheat, *Regional Growth*.

14. These data were used in Munnell, "How Does Public Infrastructure Affect Regional Economic Performance?" A recent paper by Douglas Holtz-Eakin utilizes a different set of state estimates of public-sector capital. Holtz- Eakin, "Public-Sector Capital and the Productivity Puzzle," Working Paper 4122 (Cambridge, Mass.: National Bureau of Economic Research, July 1992). Because these data provided results that were similar to those obtained with Munnell's series, the results are not reported here.

*Results*

The first four columns of table 2-5 show the results for manufacturing employment growth in each of the two periods with and without the government infrastructure variables.[15] Because $LogEMP_{t-1}$ never adds significantly to the explanation of manufacturing employment growth, it is dropped from the equations reported in table 2-5. Apparently, the agglomeration economies or diseconomies do not extend to the level of an entire state.[16]

In each equation, the *WAGE* and *UNION* variables have the expected sign, but when used together their coefficients are statistically significant in only three of eight appearances because of collinearity between these two variables. When either *WAGE* or *UNION* is dropped from the equation, the other's coefficient is negative and statistically significant in all equations. Thus labor market variables appear to have a consistent effect with the expected sign over the entire 1967–89 period. High rates of unionization and high wage rates are associated with significantly lower manufacturing employment growth.

The *TAX* and *ENERGY* variables do not fare as well.[17] *TAX* is never statistically significant and often has the wrong sign. *ENERGY* is significant only in 1977–89, but with a positive sign, suggesting that higher energy prices are *directly* related to higher manufacturing employment growth. This result is puzzling, but it recurs consistently in the results that follow.[18] The absence of significant effects from the *TAX* variable may be due to the failure of this vari-

15. The *TEMP* variable is omitted in these equations because it does not add to the explanatory power of the equations. *TEMP*, however, is used in the regressions on total nonfarm employment reported in table 2-6.

16. In the analysis of narrower metropolitan regions later, these diseconomies appear somewhat more important.

17. Some studies include a population-density variable as a proxy for land prices. This variable unfortunately does not reflect the cost of land for manufacturing facilities, nor does it add to the explanatory power of estimates of equation 2-6a, nor is it exogenous in any reasonably specified model of regional growth.

18. In recent work, Michael Wasylenko obtained the same positive relationship between energy prices and manufacturing growth across states between 1980 and 1985, but his results were statistically insignificant. See Michael Wasylenko, "Empirical Evidence on Interregional Business Location Decisions and the Role of Fiscal Incentives in Economic Development," in Henry W. Herzog, Jr., and Alan M. Schlottmann, eds., *Industry Location and Public Policy* (University of Tennessee Press, 1991), pp. 24–25.

**Table 2-5. Estimates of the Determinants of Growth in State Manufacturing Employment and Output, Selected Periods, 1967–89**[a]

| | Dependent variables | | | | | | | |
|---|---|---|---|---|---|---|---|---|
| | Δ log manufacturing employment | | | | Δ log manufacturing gross state product | | | |
| Independent variable | 1967–77 | 1967–77 | 1977–89 | 1977–89 | 1967–77 | 1967–77 | 1977–89 | 1977–89 |
| Constant | −0.10 | 0.022 | −0.51 | −0.64 | 0.42 | 0.58 | −0.26 | −0.33 |
| | (1.99) | (1.42) | (1.54) | (1.88) | (0.37) | (0.43) | (1.88) | (1.88) |
| $WAGE_{t-1}$ | −0.52 | −0.38 | −0.27 | −0.29 | −0.096 | 0.095 | −0.46 | −0.52 |
| | (1.99) | (1.42) | (1.54) | (1.88) | (0.37) | (0.43) | (1.88) | (1.88) |
| $UNION_{t-1}$ | −0.42 | −0.28 | −0.41 | −0.45 | −1.07 | −0.86 | −0.92 | −0.96 |
| | (2.04) | (1.43) | (1.72) | (2.19) | (5.68) | (4.12) | (2.53) | (2.69) |
| $TAX_{t-1}$ | 0.010 | 0.028 | −0.043 | −0.019 | 0.019 | 0.045 | 0.061 | 0.056 |
| | (0.63) | (1.28) | (1.14) | (0.60) | (1.00) | (2.06) | (1.26) | (1.20) |
| $ENERGY_{t-1}$ | 0.063 | 0.093 | 0.13 | 0.14 | −0.0069 | 0.045 | 0.19 | 0.19 |
| | (0.98) | (1.55) | (4.98) | (5.63) | (0.08) | (0.57) | (3.88) | (3.68) |
| $ZONE$ | 0.030 | 0.032 | 0.050 | 0.051 | 0.031 | 0.034 | 0.043 | 0.044 |
| | (4.16) | (5.33) | (5.32) | (6.16) | (3.47) | (4.47) | (3.40) | (3.47) |
| $MARKET_{t-1}$ | 0.18 | 0.23 | 0.043 | 0.0090 | 0.19 | 0.26 | −0.021 | −0.040 |
| | (4.54) | (4.57) | (0.75) | (0.15) | (4.29) | (4.32) | (0.20) | (0.46) |
| $MOUNTAIN\ REGION$ | 0.13 | 0.15 | 0.13 | 0.16 | −0.13 | −0.09 | 0.20 | 0.20 |
| | (2.48) | (3.08) | (3.28) | (3.60) | (1.65) | (1.19) | (3.02) | (2.80) |
| $NORTHTIER$ | −0.16 | −0.16 | −0.26 | −0.30 | −0.024 | −0.040 | −0.40 | −0.40 |
| | (2.00) | (2.05) | (6.85) | (6.70) | (0.33) | (0.54) | (4.23) | (3.91) |
| $GOVT_{t-1}$ | . . . | −0.33 | . . . | −0.10 | . . . | −0.61 | . . . | 0.049 |
| | | (0.89) | | (0.98) | | (1.55) | | (0.29) |
| $INFRA_{t-1}$ | . . . | −0.015 | . . . | 0.040 | . . . | −0.0075 | . . . | 0.0049 |
| | | (0.76) | | (2.35) | | (0.36) | | (0.21) |
| $\bar{R}^2$ | 0.821 | 0.840 | 0.766 | 0.790 | 0.720 | 0.748 | 0.590 | 0.570 |

a. The numbers in parentheses are $t$-statistics. The number of observations is 48.

able to capture marginal corporate tax rates or unmeasured tax concessions for new or expanding companies.[19]

The *ZONE* and *MARKET* variables perform very well, particularly in 1967–77, suggesting that distance from the Rust Belt and the strength of regional demand for manufactures are important in explaining manufacturing growth. However, the *ZONE* variable may be serving in part as a proxy for *UNION*, reflecting distance from heavily unionized states. When *ZONE* is dropped from the equation, the statistical significance of the coefficient of *UNION* rises markedly. Finally, *GOVT* and *INFRA* add very little to the explanatory power of the employment growth equations in 1967–77. *INFRA* assumes a significant and positive coefficient only in 1977–89 in the employment growth equation.

Equation 2-6a may also be estimated for the growth in gross state product from manufacturing as estimated by the Bureau of Economic Analysis of the Department of Commerce. The right-hand side of table 2-5 reflects these estimates. It is quite clear that *UNION* is related much more strongly (and inversely) to manufacturing output growth than to employment growth. Otherwise, the results on the right-hand side of table 2-5 generally mirror those on the left-hand side. The only exceptions are the negative effect of *MOUNTAIN REGION* in the 1967–77 output regressions and the absence of a significant coefficient of *INFRA* in the 1977–89 output regressions.

The results in table 2-5 thus decisively support the theory that labor market variables are very important in manufacturing growth across states. State taxation has little perceptible effect at this level of aggregation over 1967–89, and measures of government spending and infrastructure are generally unimportant. Unexplained are the generally superior performance of the mountain states and the seemingly perverse effect of energy prices after 1977.

Extending the period of analysis into the 1990–91 recession (not shown) has one important effect. The tax variable has a statistically

19. Some corroboration of this surmise may be found in a recent paper by Leslie E. Papke, who estimates the effects of taxes, wages, and other variables on new establishments in five manufacturing industries, calculating effective state tax rates for each industry. She finds that state taxes have a significant negative effect on new establishment births in three of five industries, but that wages generally have a larger negative effect. See Leslie E. Papke, "Interstate Business Tax Differentials and New Firm Location: Evidence from Panel Data," Working Paper 3184 (Cambridge, Mass.: National Bureau of Economic Research, November 1989).

Table 2-6. Estimates of the Determinants of Growth in Nonfarm Employment and Total Gross State Product, Selected Periods, 1967–89[a]

| | Dependent variables | | | | | | | |
| --- | --- | --- | --- | --- | --- | --- | --- | --- |
| | Δ log nonfarm employment | | | | Δ log gross state product | | | |
| Independent variable | 1967–77 | 1967–77 | 1977–89 | 1977–89 | 1967–77 | 1967–77 | 1977–89 | 1977–89 |
| Constant | 0.17 | 0.14 | −0.27 | −0.38 | 0.076 | 0.093 | −0.39 | −0.42 |
| | (0.13) | (0.06) | (0.22) | (0.03) | (0.13) | (0.22) | (0.97) | (0.60) |
| $WAGE_{t-1}$ | 0.018 | 0.0093 | 0.042 | −0.0068 | −0.020 | 0.033 | −0.20 | −0.16 |
| | (0.13) | (0.06) | (0.22) | (0.03) | (0.13) | (0.22) | (0.97) | (0.60) |
| $UNION_{t-1}$ | −0.50 | −0.49 | −0.29 | −0.32 | −0.32 | −0.22 | −0.15 | −0.12 |
| | (3.55) | (3.47) | (1.33) | (1.55) | (2.28) | (1.45) | (0.56) | (0.45) |
| $TAX_{t-1}$ | −0.032 | −0.052 | 0.0005 | 0.010 | −0.0074 | 0.0029 | 0.053 | 0.072 |
| | (2.13) | (2.39) | (0.01) | (0.30) | (0.38) | (0.15) | (1.18) | (1.61) |
| $ENERGY_{t-1}$ | 0.069 | 0.082 | 0.14 | 0.14 | 0.11 | 0.15 | 0.19 | 0.19 |
| | (1.67) | (1.92) | (5.07) | (5.00) | (1.57) | (2.08) | (4.91) | (4.85) |
| ZONE | 0.018 | 0.018 | 0.017 | 0.016 | 0.019 | 0.019 | 0.012 | 0.011 |
| | (4.16) | (4.10) | (1.66) | (1.79) | (4.39) | (4.40) | (1.00) | (0.96) |
| $MARKET_{t-1}$ | 0.016 | 0.012 | 0.032 | 0.010 | −0.022 | −0.0059 | −0.044 | −0.043 |
| | (0.60) | (0.40) | (0.48) | (0.14) | (0.67) | (0.15) | (0.49) | (0.41) |
| MOUNTAIN REGION | 0.14 | 0.14 | 0.12 | 0.13 | 0.13 | 0.15 | 0.18 | 0.19 |
| | (5.23) | (4.99) | (3.61) | (3.91) | (3.27) | (3.58) | (4.53) | (4.74) |
| NORTHTIER | 0.013 | −0.024 | −0.20 | −0.22 | −0.063 | −0.090 | −0.23 | −0.24 |
| | (0.51) | (0.01) | (4.89) | (5.67) | (1.37) | (1.73) | (5.73) | (4.18) |
| $GOVT_{t-1}$ | ... | −0.012 | ... | −0.017 | ... | −0.041 | ... | −0.11 |
| | | (0.56) | | (0.18) | | (1.76) | | (0.92) |
| $INFRA_{t-1}$ | ... | 0.013 | ... | 0.020 | ... | 0.018 | ... | 0.019 |
| | | (1.21) | | (1.56) | | (1.24) | | (1.18) |
| TEMP | 0.0028 | 0.0030 | 0.0029 | 0.0034 | 0.0030 | 0.0032 | 0.0051 | 0.0034 |
| | (3.21) | (3.42) | (2.01) | (2.24) | (2.96) | (5.16) | (2.05) | (2.20) |
| $\bar{R}^2$ | 0.818 | 0.813 | 0.565 | 0.564 | 0.584 | 0.582 | 0.548 | 0.531 |

a. The numbers in parentheses are t-statistics. The number of observations is 48.

significant coefficient in the employment equation, but all other coefficients are similar to those reported in table 2-5. Thus the estimated influence of taxes appears to depend somewhat on the period chosen for analysis, but the estimated labor market coefficients are robust across the various periods.

For purposes of comparison, I also estimated equation 2-6a for nonfarm employment and total gross state product. These results, shown in table 2-6, are broadly similar to those for the manufacturing sector. Nonfarm employment growth is less precisely related to labor market variables than is manufacturing growth, and *TAX* is significant at modest confidence levels in 1967–77. *MARKET* is not related to nonfarm employment growth, suggesting that its effects on manufacturing are too small to influence the much broader domain of nonfarm employment. The *GOVT* and *INFRA* variables perform even more poorly in explaining nonfarm employment growth than in explaining manufacturing employment growth. Weather is clearly related to nonfarm employment and total output, undoubtedly due to its effect on population migration. Otherwise, the estimates are at least qualitatively similar to those for the manufacturing sector.[20]

The results of the empirical analysis of state data thus point to labor market variables as the most persistent influences on differential growth rates, particularly in manufacturing. The degree of unionization and, to a somewhat lesser extent, wage rates are inversely related to employment and output growth in manufacturing. Government spending, infrastructure, and tax variables are less important at this level of aggregation. In addition, the mountain region and the distance from the Rust Belt are directly related to manufacturing growth. The only apparently perverse result emerging from the state data is the persistently direct effect of energy prices on growth after 1977.[21]

20. Because labor demand and supply are both likely to be influenced by the price of labor, a simultaneous-equation model in which population growth, employment growth, and the rental price of human capital are endogenous was estimated using climate (*TEMP*), government expenditures, and infrastructure as exogenous instruments. The resulting coefficient estimates for the exogenous variables are so similar to those reported in tables 2-5 and 2-6 that they are not reported. The only major differences appear in 1977–89 for total nonfarm employment. But for manufacturing employment, there are no important differences in coefficient estimates for the major structural variables.

21. Very similar results are obtained from alternative functional forms of equation 2-6a. Log-log and linear specifications do not yield results that are very different

### Metropolitan Areas

The state data used thus far represent an aggregation over potentially dissimilar areas—Los Angeles and Eureka, California, for instance. More precise estimates of the importance of various economic forces in stimulating manufacturing growth may be available in an analysis of metropolitan areas. The Bureau of Labor Statistics provides estimates of sectoral employment by areas that roughly correspond to metropolitan statistical areas. Unfortunately, data on infrastructure are not available by labor market area, nor are state and local government expenditures. The average manufacturing wage (*WAGERATE*) is available, as is state and local tax effort for 1967 and 1977. Because I cannot adjust the metropolitan area wage variable for labor quality, I include a separate variable for education (*EDUCATION*)—the median years of schooling for males from the Census of Population.[22] For unionization, I use the share of union membership in nonfarm employment for the entire state. Similarly, I use the state data on energy prices. The *TAX* variable is the ACIR's measure of the states' effort to tax corporations' capacity. The ACIR's measure of overall tax effort by metropolitan statistical area is available only for 1967 and does not perform very well. Complete data are available for 100 comparable areas over the 1967–77 period and for 150 areas for 1977–89. The results are shown in table 2-7.

The analyses of state and metropolitan areas once again point to the importance of labor market variables, unionization, and wages, and distance from the Rust Belt in explaining the growth or decline in manufacturing output and employment. *UNION* is more important in the earlier period, while *WAGERATE* performs better in the later period. Once again, *TAX* does not add significantly to the explanation of 1967–77 growth, but surprisingly it is directly related to employment growth in the later period.

There is some evidence in the labor market analysis of negative

---

from those reported in table 2-5 for the semilogarithmic specifications. Thus the results reported herein are not driven by the specific functional form used in the analysis.

22. The education variable is drawn from the 1970 census for 1967–89 and from the 1980 census for 1977–89. Bureau of the Census, *Census of Population* (Department of Commerce, 1970, 1980).

**Table 2-7. Estimates of Manufacturing Employment Growth in Labor Market Areas, Selected Periods, 1967–89[a]**

| | Dependent variable ($\Delta$log employment) | | | |
|---|---|---|---|---|
| | 1967–77 | | 1977–89 | |
| Independent variable | Without regional dummies | With regional dummies | Without regional dummies | With regional dummies |
| Constant | 0.46 | 0.11 | −5.07 | −4.79 |
| $LogEMP_{t-1}$ | −0.059 | −0.058 | −0.011 | −0.0094 |
| | (3.66) | (4.04) | (0.61) | (0.52) |
| $WAGERATE_{t-1}$ | 0.0032 | 0.0028 | −0.12 | −0.13 |
| | (1.10) | (0.97) | (5.00) | (4.64) |
| $UNION_{t-1}$ | −1.00 | −0.88 | −0.34 | −0.55 |
| | (4.79) | (2.30) | (1.52) | (1.20) |
| $EDUCATION_{t-1}$ | 0.022 | 0.018 | 0.45 | 0.43 |
| | (0.59) | (0.41) | (6.32) | (6.17) |
| $TAX_{t-1}$ | −0.018 | −0.011 | 0.97 | 0.62 |
| | (0.74) | (0.16) | (1.84) | (1.17) |
| $ENERGY_{t-1}$ | −0.25 | −0.029 | 0.023 | 0.041 |
| | (1.64) | (0.18) | (0.36) | (0.54) |
| ZONE | 0.023 | 0.037 | 0.027 | 0.033 |
| | (3.70) | (1.97) | (2.97) | (1.78) |
| $\bar{R}^2$ | 0.543 | 0.618 | 0.482 | 0.495 |
| $n$ | 100 | 100 | 150 | 150 |

a. The numbers in parentheses are $t$-statistics.

agglomeration effects. In 1967–77, manufacturing employment growth is inversely related to the number of manufacturing employees in the area in 1967. Thus in this period a large local manufacturing base appears to be a disadvantage. These negative agglomeration effects disappear in the later period. In both periods, distance from the Rust Belt (*ZONE*) is directly and significantly related to manufacturing growth.

## The Role of Infrastructure and Government Spending

The literature on regional growth devotes considerable attention to the effects of state and local government spending policies and infrastructure on the growth of employment or the attraction of new industry. Bartik finds that approximately 60 percent of the studies of regional growth reveal a positive association of some measure of government spending or infrastructure with state or local business growth.[23] Munnell finds a significant relationship between infrastructure and state employment growth, and I have used her infrastructure measures in this chapter.[24]

In order to examine the effects of state and local government spending and infrastructure more carefully, I divided spending into four categories—health, education, welfare, and other—and infrastructure into three—highways, water systems and sewers, and other.[25] I deflated each by the state's population as in table 2-4. When these more detailed variables were substituted for *GOVT* and *INFRA* in the equations reported in tables 2-5 and 2-6, only a few added to the explanatory power of the regression equations. Of the public spending variables, welfare expenditures are inversely related to growth in all of the nonfarm employment and total output growth equations, but in only one-fourth of the manufacturing equations. Other expenditures are directly related to the growth in nonfarm employment and total gross state product in the later period. Similarly, infrastructure other than highways and water resource investments is driving the positive coefficient on *INFRA* in the 1977–89 manufacturing equation, perhaps reflecting such investments as schools or government correctional facilities. Otherwise, there is little to suggest that infrastructure levels or government expenditures in such important areas as education add to the ability to explain the growth in employment or gross product.

### Alternative Tax Measures

Given the poor performance of the tax variable in the results reported above, I experimented with other measures of the intensity of state taxation. First, I used ACIR's measure of the states' overall tax effort. Second, I used William Wheaton's estimate of each state's business and manufacturing tax rate for 1977.[26] Finally, I used total

23. Bartik, *Who Benefits*, p. 47.

24. Munnell, "How Does Public Infrastructure Affect Regional Economic Performance?"

25. These latter three categories are those used by Munnell.

26. William C. Wheaton, "Interstate Differences in the Level of Business Taxation," *National Tax Journal*, vol. 36 (March 1983), pp. 83–94.

tax collections per dollar of state personal income and total corporate tax collections per dollar of gross state product from manufacturing. None of the coefficients of these variables was statistically significant for the manufacturing employment or manufacturing output equations in either period.

### High-tech versus Low-tech Industries

Given the importance of high-technology industries to the future of U.S. manufacturing, it might be interesting to see if these industries are attracted by the same microeconomic variables as the low-technology industries. The division of industries into high-tech and low-tech is generally based upon research and development intensity. Most of the high-tech manufacturing industries are in the two-digit census classifications of chemicals, machinery, electrical machinery, and instruments.[27] Aerospace (SIC 372) is also in this category, but it is included in the two-digit industry, transportation equipment (SIC 37), which is dominated by motor vehicles. Because comparable state data are difficult to obtain for three- or four-digit industries, I included only the aforementioned four two-digit industries in high-tech and relegated the rest to low-tech and estimated equation 2-6a on each subset for census employment data in 1967–77 and 1977–87.

The results for both subsets are qualitatively similar to those reported in table 2-5 for all manufacturing employment; however, the high-tech industries are twice as responsive to differences in *UNION* and *WAGE* as the low-tech industries. This may be a reflection of the greater mobility of high-tech industries in general. High-tech industry employment growth is not related to public infrastructure or to energy prices in 1977–89, but the low-tech industries' growth is directly related to both variables in this period. In the earlier period, the energy price coefficient is statistically significant with a *negative* sign for the high-tech industries, but not for the low-tech industries. The *TAX* variable's coefficient continues to be statistically insignificant for both sets of industries in both time periods.

27. Regina Kelly, "The Impact of Technological Innovation on Trade Patterns," ER–24 (Department of Commerce, Bureau of International Economic Policy and Research, December 1977).

## Corroborative Evidence from Individual Industries

The results for the entire manufacturing sector suggest rather strongly that unionization, wage rates, and distance from the Rust Belt explain a substantial share of the variance in the growth of the states' manufacturing activity. If these results are correct, they should also be observable in the growth of individual manufacturing industries.

Census and BLS data on individual manufacturing industries by state are available for two-digit industries for most states but not for less aggregated three- or four-digit industries. Even the two-digit employment and value-added data are not available for many industries in the smaller states; hence my analysis is confined to the larger states for much of what follows.

There are two ways of examining the trends by two-digit industries across states. First, it is possible to analyze the growth rates in each state across the twenty two-digit industries. This may be accomplished by simply estimating separate regressions for each state relating the change in employment or in output on state-specific measures of the independent variables. A second approach is to estimate the regressions reported in tables 2-5 and 2-6 for each two-digit industry across all states. Both approaches yield mildly corroborative conclusions.

The first approach requires data for each industry in each state. Since corporate tax rates or energy prices do not vary by industry within a state, it is impossible to include them in individual state regressions. Wage rate data are available by industry and state, however, and the attractiveness of an industry's wage in a given state may be indicated by the level of that wage relative to the U.S. average for the industry. In addition, I include the national degree of unionization of an industry to see whether a state is gaining or losing unionized industries, ceteris paribus.

I estimated individual state regressions across nineteen industries for the larger states, including all middle Atlantic and east north central states plus Massachusetts, North Carolina, Florida, Texas, California, and Oregon. If high relative wage rates and unionization are responsible for a large share of the decline in Rust Belt manufacturing, one should expect to see negative coefficients on all relative wage variables but positive coefficients on the unionization variable for states that offer a lower probability of union or-

**Table 2-8. Estimates of the Relationship between Manufacturing
Employment Growth and Relative Wages and Unionization in Selected
Large Industrial States[a]**

| State | Dependent variable (ΔLog in employment, 1967–89) | | |
| | $RELWAGE_{t-1}$ | $UNION_{t-1}$ | Number of industries |
| --- | --- | --- | --- |
| Illinois | −2.76 | −0.86 | 19 |
| | (1.98) | (1.44) | |
| Indiana | −2.21 | −1.98 | 17 |
| | (1.78) | (3.32) | |
| Michigan | −0.66 | −0.85 | 18 |
| | (0.88) | (1.26) | |
| Ohio | −1.59 | −1.39 | 15 |
| | (2.04) | (2.98) | |
| Wisconsin | −4.35 | −0.44 | 18 |
| | (2.32) | (0.63) | |
| New Jersey | −2.03 | −1.65 | 19 |
| | (1.34) | (2.09) | |
| New York | −1.08 | −1.35 | 18 |
| | (0.97) | (2.05) | |
| Pennsylvania | −4.53 | −0.65 | 19 |
| | (1.85) | (0.95) | |
| Massachusetts | −4.65 | −1.25 | 16 |
| | (2.41) | (1.59) | |
| North Carolina | −2.43 | 0.25 | 15 |
| | (2.62) | (0.33) | |
| Florida | −2.32 | −1.95 | 18 |
| | (2.08) | (2.68) | |
| Texas | −0.58 | 0.18 | 17 |
| | (0.40) | (0.18) | |
| California | −0.61 | −2.19 | 18 |
| | (0.70) | (4.42) | |
| Oregon | −0.46 | −0.53 | 17 |
| | (0.40) | (0.46) | |

a. Numbers in parentheses are *t*-statistics.

ganization and negative coefficients on those variables for the
unionized Rust Belt states.

The results for each of the fourteen states examined appear in
table 2-8, reported for 1967–89. In every state, the coefficient of the
relative wage variable (*RELWAGE*) is negative, and in all northern
industrial states the coefficients of the unionization variable are also
negative. The expected positive coefficients for the unionization variable appear for North Carolina and Texas but not for Florida or the
two western states. The results are not generally as robust as those

for manufacturing in general, suggesting that the simple two-variable analysis suffers from the problem of omitted variables.

A more satisfying approach is to look at each industry separately, repeating the empirical analysis reported for the entire manufacturing sector in table 2-5 above. I estimated cross-sectional regressions of the determinants of employment and output change for sixteen of the twenty two-digit industries for which sufficient state data were available. In these regressions, an industry-specific wage rate and a variable reflecting the share of men with a high school education in the labor force were substituted for the human capital–adjusted wage rate.[28]

In twenty-eight of thirty-two regressions, at least one labor market variable was statistically significant with the expected sign. In the 1967–77 regressions, there were only five of sixteen industries that did not have a significant labor market coefficient. The coefficients for *WAGERATE* were negative and significant in nine of the sixteen industries in 1977–87, most of which are durable-goods industries. Of the other variables, only *ENERGY*, *ZONE*, and *MOUNTAIN REGION* contributed much to explaining two-digit industry employment growth in 1967–77 and had the expected signs. In the 1977–87 period, the coefficients of *ENERGY* were positive once again in three industries. The infrastructure and government spending variables were rarely important in explaining industry employment growth. The coefficients of *INFRA* were positive and significant in only two of sixteen industries in each of the two periods. The coefficients of *GOVT* were negative and significant in only three of the thirty-two industry regressions; they were never positive and significant. For some reason, the coefficients of *INFRA* were significant in both periods for the food processing industry.

## New Plants, Expansions, Contractions, and Closures

Thus far I have focused solely on the net growth of employment and output in manufacturing and the larger nonfarm economy. This growth is the result of new establishment formation and the expan-

28. The *WAGERATE* variables are obtained from wages and hours worked as reported in the 1967 and 1977 *Census of Manufactures*. The employment data are also drawn from the *Census of Manufactures* because the census data for two-digit manufacturing industries are much more complete than the BLS data.

sion of existing establishments, as well as establishment closures and contractions. Given the concern over plant closings and the attraction of new industries, it is desirable to break down the growth in employment or output into four categories: new establishments; expansion of existing establishments; contractions of existing establishments; and establishment closures.

The Census Bureau provides employment and output data for current establishments, but these data provide no information on the number of new or closed establishments or on expansions or contractions of establishments in existence at the time of the previous quinquennial census. However, the Census Bureau also has a Longitudinal Research Database (LRD) that links annual Surveys of Manufactures and thereby tracks establishments, identifying expansions, contractions, and closures. New establishments are added to this data base by using census reports on new establishments in multiunit companies and employer identification numbers for single-establishment companies from the Social Security Administration.[29]

The LRD data have been tabulated for the census regions by Steve Davis and John Haltiwanger, but only for job creation (expansions and new births) and job destruction (contractions and closures) in manufacturing. These data are shown as annual averages for 1973–86 in table 2-9. Note that the job creation rates exhibit more variance than the destruction rates, suggesting that regional employment growth varies more because of differences in new establishment formation or expansions than because of differences in plant closings and contractions.[30] The Rust Belt states grow less rapidly than southern or western states because they have substantially lower rates of job formation, not because of much higher rates of job losses due to closures or contractions. In fact, the higher rate of expansion in the West leads to a somewhat higher rate of contraction as well. New ventures are more likely to fail than established enterprises.

More detailed data on job creation and destruction are available

29. For a description of these data, see Steven J. Davis and John Haltiwanger, "Gross Job Creation, Gross Job Destruction, and Employment Reallocation," *Quarterly Journal of Economics*, vol. 107 (August 1992), pp. 819–63.

30. The same result was found by Catherine Armington, Candee Harris, and Marjorie Odle in "Formation and Growth in High Technology Businesses: A Regional Assessment" (Brookings, Business Microdata Project, September 30, 1983).

**Table 2-9. Annual Rates of Manufacturing Employment Creation and Destruction as a Share of Regional Employment, 1973–86**
Percent

| Region | Creation | Destruction |
|--------|----------|-------------|
| New England | 9.2 | 9.9 |
| Middle Atlantic | 8.4 | 11.2 |
| East north central | 8.1 | 10.3 |
| West north central | 9.3 | 9.7 |
| South Atlantic | 8.9 | 9.3 |
| East south central | 9.0 | 9.7 |
| West south central | 10.3 | 10.5 |
| Mountain | 11.8 | 10.1 |
| Pacific | 12.0 | 11.5 |

Source: Data supplied by John Haltiwanger.

**Table 2-10. Employment Creation in Manufacturing from New Plants, Expansions, Contractions, and Closures, Selected Periods, 1976–88**
Millions of jobs per year

| Period | New plants | Expansions | Contractions | Plant closures |
|--------|-----------|-----------|-------------|----------------|
| 1976–78 | 1.26 | 1.43 | −0.82 | −1.17 |
| 1978–80 | 0.93 | 1.07 | −0.72 | −0.70 |
| 1980–82 | 0.89 | 1.03 | −1.02 | −1.60 |
| 1982–84[a] | 1.05 | 0.79 | −0.79 | −1.11 |
| 1984–86 | 1.48 | 0.92 | −0.86 | −1.55 |
| 1986–88 | 2.03 | 0.82 | −0.58 | −1.84 |

Source: Small Business Administration, Office of Advocacy, State Patterns of Employment Growth data.
a. Excludes Illinois and Texas (missing data for 1982–84).

from the Small Business Administration, based largely on Dun and Bradstreet data. The SBA presents regional tabulations for new plants, expansions, contractions, and plant closures for all nonfarm sectors, including manufacturing (table 2-10). Consistent data are available for 1976–88, and they also show that the important difference between the Rust Belt states and the South and West lies in their much lower job growth due to the birth of new establishments, not to a higher rate of job losses due to plant closures (table 2-11).[31]

The SBA data are cumulated from biennial reports for 1976–78 through 1986–88.[32] A comparison of 1976–80 with 1980–88 pro-

31. These data have been criticized as being less accurate than the census data because of difficulties involved in separating births and deaths from acquisitions or sales of existing plants, but they paint very much the same picture as the census data.

32. SBA officials admit that there is some potential for overstatement of net job creation and destruction in their data because of their inability to be sure that the

Table 2-11. Average Annual Rates of Employment Changes from New Plants, Expansions, Contractions, and Closures as a Share of Manufacturing Employment, 1976–80 and 1980–88

Percent

| Region | New plants | | Expansions | | Contractions | | Plant closures | |
|---|---|---|---|---|---|---|---|---|
| | 1976–80 | 1980–88 | 1976–80 | 1980–88 | 1976–80 | 1980–88 | 1976–80 | 1980–88 |
| New England | 4.9 | 6.2 | 7.6 | 4.3 | −4.7 | −4.1 | −4.8 | −7.6 |
| Middle Atlantic | 4.4 | 6.7 | 5.2 | 3.7 | −4.3 | −4.0 | −5.0 | −7.5 |
| East north central | 5.4 | 5.9[a] | 5.4 | 4.0[a] | −4.0 | −4.6[a] | −4.6 | −6.9[a] |
| West north central | 5.1 | 6.0 | 7.0 | 4.5 | −4.3 | −4.2 | −3.9 | −6.5 |
| South Atlantic | 5.5 | 7.4 | 6.3 | 4.7 | −3.3 | −3.4 | −5.0 | −7.6 |
| East south central | 5.6 | 7.1 | 5.8 | 4.2 | −3.5 | −3.6 | −4.3 | −7.6 |
| West south central | 8.1 | 6.0[b] | 8.9 | 4.5[b] | −3.7 | −4.2[b] | −5.1 | −6.5[b] |
| Mountain | 8.6 | 9.0 | 9.1 | 6.5 | −4.5 | −4.1 | −5.1 | −9.5 |
| Pacific | 8.0 | 8.3 | 9.3 | 6.0 | −4.2 | −4.3 | −6.2 | −9.1 |

Source: Small Business Administration, Office of Advocacy, State Patterns of Employment Growth data.
a. Excludes Illinois (missing data for 1982–84).
b. Excludes Texas (missing data for 1982–84).

**Table 2-12. Estimates of the Determinants of Growth Rates in Manufacturing from New Plants, Expansions, Contractions, and Closures across States, 1976–88[a]**

Dependent variable: log (employment growth/manufacturing employment)[b]

| Independent variable | New plants | | Expansions | | Contractions | | Closures | |
|---|---|---|---|---|---|---|---|---|
| Constant | 6.29 | 5.79 | 5.76 | 5.34 | 5.84 | 5.45 | 6.91 | 6.46 |
| WAGERATE | −0.02 | −0.078 | −0.13 | −0.23 | −0.14 | −0.14 | −0.10 | −0.17 |
| | (0.37) | (1.46) | (2.12) | (4.53) | (2.56) | (2.16) | (1.61) | (2.59) |
| UNION | −1.03 | 0.045 | −0.97 | 0.30 | 0.99 | 0.78 | −0.007 | 0.011 |
| | (2.24) | (0.10) | (1.88) | (0.74) | (0.24) | (1.60) | (0.02) | (2.31) |
| EDUCATION | 0.68 | 1.34 | 1.61 | 2.50 | 1.36 | 2.00 | 0.81 | 1.73 |
| | (1.38) | (3.43) | (3.17) | (6.21) | (2.79) | (4.09) | (1.62) | (4.20) |
| TAX | −0.58 | −1.21 | 0.095 | −0.023 | −0.71 | −1.03 | 0.034 | −0.54 |
| | (1.17) | (2.13) | (1.51) | (0.43) | (1.37) | (2.12) | (0.44) | (0.69) |
| ENERGY | 0.038 | 0.19 | −0.059 | 0.11 | −0.09 | −0.0087 | −0.15 | −0.0078 |
| | (0.59) | (3.25) | (0.87) | (2.50) | (1.79) | (0.17) | (2.11) | (0.12) |
| ZONE | 0.023 | 0.052 | 0.030 | 0.068 | −0.0054 | 0.010 | −0.007 | 0.022 |
| | (1.58) | (3.82) | (2.11) | (5.96) | (0.46) | (0.79) | (0.43) | (1.27) |

| | (1) | (2) | (3) | (4) | (5) | (6) | (7) | (8) |
|---|---|---|---|---|---|---|---|---|
| MARKET | 0.045 | 0.12 | 0.20 | 0.20 | 0.26 | 0.41 | 0.11 | 0.19 |
| | (0.44) | (0.75) | (1.96) | (1.82) | (2.85) | (3.46) | (0.85) | (1.02) |
| MOUNTAIN REGION | 0.58 | 0.28 | 0.078 | −0.009 | −0.20 | −0.32 | 0.30 | 0.18 |
| | (2.69) | (2.33) | (0.77) | (0.13) | (1.70) | (3.31) | (2.10) | (1.42) |
| NORTHTIER | −0.27 | −0.24 | −0.11 | 0.006 | 0.10 | 0.11 | −0.087 | 0.00093 |
| | (2.32) | (1.73) | (1.38) | (0.05) | (1.06) | (1.04) | (0.65) | (0.0049) |
| METALSH | 0.22 | −0.089 | 0.89 | 0.66 | 1.06 | 0.74 | 0.29 | 0.00094 |
| | (1.01) | (0.34) | (3.29) | (3.28) | (4.42) | (3.83) | (0.90) | (0.00028) |
| GOVT | ... | 0.017 | ... | 0.018 | ... | 0.014 | ... | 0.023 |
| | | (0.95) | | (5.12) | | (1.98) | | (3.43) |
| INFRA | ... | −0.046 | ... | −0.069 | ... | −0.061 | ... | −0.079 |
| | | (1.98) | | (4.28) | | (3.55) | | (5.74) |
| $\bar{R}^2$ | 0.498 | 0.624 | 0.626 | 0.785 | 0.450 | 0.593 | 0.326 | 0.444 |
| $n$ | 48 | 46 | 48 | 46 | 48 | 46 | 48 | 46 |

a. The numbers in parentheses are $t$-statistics.
b. The dependent variable is the logarithm of the *absolute value* of employment growth as a share of 1976 manufacturing employment.

vides more insight into the apparently sharp decline in the central regions noted by Branson and Love during the second period, when the dollar was strong (table 2-11).[33] The closure rates do indeed rise in all of the central divisions, but by no more than in the other regions. For existing enterprises, however, the central regions show a somewhat larger decline in the expansion rate and a larger rise in the contraction rate than do the coastal and mountain regions. Thus the SBA data seem to point to expansions and contractions, not closures, as the villains in the central regions' relative decline during the early and mid-1980s.

The SBA data may be used to estimate the effects of microeconomic variables on each component of the job creation or destruction process. The results of regressing the rate of employment creation and destruction in each category on the variables appearing in equation 2-6a are shown in table 2-12. In addition to the variables used previously, I include a measure of the share of manufacturing employment accounted for by metals and metal-fabricating industries (*METALSH*). The *WAGERATE* variable is the average wage rate in manufacturing. The *EDUCATION* variable is the share of men with a high school education.

Perhaps the most surprising result at first blush is the role of the metals-related industries, *METALSH*, which contribute both to job gains from expansion and to job losses from contractions. Given the shift of employment in such industries as steel, automobiles, machine tools, and heavy equipment, this result may be understandable. Large steel plants and Big Three automobile assembly plants have been operating at low capacity utilization while minimills and transplant automobile assembly have been growing in many of the same states.

The labor market variables work very well in explaining the two components of job creation—new plants and plant expansions—but less well in explaining job losses due to closures or contractions. Since the dependent variable in the last four columns of table 2-12 is the absolute rate of job destruction, a negative coefficient in these columns implies that a higher value of the variable is associated with less job *destruction*. Thus the significant negative coefficients

---

Dun and Bradstreet data on which they are based have discarded all closed or acquired establishments.

33. See discussion of Branson and Love's study in chapter 1.

for wages in the contractions equations are a puzzle. It is far from clear why high wages should reduce the rate of contraction unless industries such as steel and autos in high-wage states tend to have strong employment-protection provisions in their labor contracts.

The contractions and closures equations are inversely related to the per capita level of public infrastructure, providing perhaps the first significant evidence of the importance of this variable. Apparently, infrastructure is important in preventing plants from partially or fully closing but not in attracting new plants or new investments in existing ones.

The results in table 2-12 generally confirm the earlier results of analysis of the net effect of all of the components of the job creation and destruction process. It is perhaps not surprising that the microeconomic variables are better able to explain the creation of new employment from plant openings and expansions than from plant closures or contractions in which a large share of costs are sunk.

## The Effects of Environmental Policy

Environmental policy is generally ignored in empirical analyses of geographical location. This may be an important but understandable omission, given the practical difficulties in measuring the effects of environmental policy.

Standards for water pollution, air pollution, land use, or solid waste disposal vary across states and even within states. For many pollutants, these differences are mandated by federal law. Federal statutes give the Environmental Protection Agency wide latitude in establishing technology-based standards for new or existing sources of pollution. For instance, the Clean Air Act requires the EPA to set tight new-source standards for many pollutants and even more onerous procedures and standards for areas that do not meet minimum air quality requirements.[34] States are allowed to devise their own plans for meeting these standards, but only within the guidelines established by the EPA.

There are no comprehensive indexes of the burdens of environmental regulation; there are only data on estimated total compliance costs, and even these data may be subject to substantial error,

34. See Robert W. Crandall, *Controlling Industrial Pollution: The Economics and Politics of Clean Air* (Brookings, 1983), pp. 8–9, 14–15.

given the difficulty in separating ordinary production costs from pollution control costs. Even if they are accurate, however, estimated total compliance costs do not provide a measure of the regulation-induced incremental cost of expanding output at an existing plant or of the environmental requirements—including lengthy licensing delays—of building new plants. Indeed, if the latter are large enough, no new plants will be built, and recorded costs will be zero.

Nevertheless, the census data on environmental compliance costs for manufacturing may be used to gauge at least an approximate effect of environmental policy on the geographic location of manufacturing. The census data include both capital investment in new pollution control equipment and total operating costs for all pollution control facilities, reported by state. Because these data do not exist for years before 1973, it is impossible to construct a capital stock measure for pollution control equipment. Therefore, I use only the operating cost data, including accounting charges for depreciation expense, as the measure of control costs.[35] These operating costs for the entire manufacturing sector for each state are divided by current-dollar estimates of gross state manufacturing output to provide an estimate of the relative importance of pollution control costs.[36] Because the compliance data are unavailable for the 1960s, I focus my analysis on 1977–91, using control costs per dollar of output in 1977.[37]

One might expect environmental control costs to be highest in the dirty, old, northern industrial states. However, because of the more stringent control of new sources, control costs per dollar of manufacturing output are 60 percent higher in the West and twice as high in the South as in the North. It is small wonder, therefore,

35. These data also include payments to government by manufacturers for pollution abatement. Expenditures for abatement or disposal of air pollutants, water pollutants, and solid waste are included. All data are in current dollars. See Bureau of the Census, "Pollution Abatement Cost and Expenditures," *Current Industrial Reports*, annual editions.

36. Data on control costs by individual industry are not available for a large number of states and industries. Therefore I do not attempt to relate individual industry growth to industry-specific control costs.

37. As explained later, I also use this variable in extending the analysis of relative employment growth due to plant starts, expansions, contractions, and closures during 1976–88.

**Table 2-13. The Effect of Pollution Control Costs on Manufacturing Employment Growth**[a]

Elasticity of employment growth

| Period and source | With infrastructure and government spending variables | Without infrastructure and government spending variables |
|---|---|---|
| *Period* | *Manufacturing employment* | |
| 1977–89 | −0.02 | −0.03 |
| | (1.01) | (1.06) |
| 1977–91 | −0.03 | −0.04 |
| | (1.39) | (1.31) |
| | | |
| *Source* | *New plants, expansions, contractions, closures*[b] | |
| New plants | −0.07 | −0.07 |
| | (1.25) | (1.28) |
| Expansions | −0.15 | −0.14 |
| | (4.37) | (2.96) |
| Contractions | 0.17 | 0.12 |
| | (6.23) | (2.61) |
| Closures | 0.05 | 0.04 |
| | (0.75) | (0.60) |

Source: Author's calculations. The unit of observation is the state. There are 48 observations.
a. Numbers in parentheses are *t*-statistics.
b. 1976–88.

that the political support for environmental policies is generally stronger in the North than in the South or West.[38]

When pollution control operating costs per dollar of output are added as an independent variable to equation 2-6a, they are not statistically significant in either 1977–89 or 1977–91 (see table 2-13). Thus compliance costs per se do not seem to have a measurable effect on the regional distribution of manufacturing employment.

Perhaps more interesting is the effect of environmental control costs on plant startups, expansions, contractions, and closures. The bottom half of table 2-13 reports the results from including compliance costs in the regressions involving these more disaggregated sources of employment growth (reported in table 2-12). New plants or plant closures do not appear to be affected by these control costs, but employment growth from *both* expansions and closures is affected by these costs. The growth in employment from plant expansions is inversely related to compliance costs. More surprisingly,

38. See League of Conservation Voters, *How Congress Voted on Energy and the Environment* (Washington: LCV, annual editions).

employment declines from closures are also reduced by high compliance costs. (The elasticity of employment growth with respect to
pollution costs is positive because higher costs reduce employment
declines due to plant contractions.) These results suggest that plant
turnover is reduced by high compliance costs, slowing contractions
in a state as well as reducing expansions.

Thus pollution control spending may not have major effects on
the overall regional distribution of manufacturing employment, but
it appears to slow industrial plant growth and decline. One should
not conclude from this analysis, however, that environmental policy
does not affect plant start-ups because reported compliance costs
from plants that are never built are likely to be small indeed.

## Comparisons with Previous Research

The empirical literature on the determinants of regional growth
has expanded considerably in the past few years. Before the mid–
1980s, most empirical studies employed rather simple regression
techniques on cross-sectional employment or output data, using
states or metropolitan areas as the units of observation. Wheat's
early research and even his 1986 study are perhaps the best example
of such research.[39] Other early studies using cross-sectional techniques on state data include those by Thomas Plaut and Joseph
Pluta and Robert Newman.[40] All three studies find a statistically
significant and negative effect of unionization, but none finds an
effect of the relative wage.[41] Wheat finds no effect of state tax policy,

39. Wheat, *Regional Growth*; and Leonard F. Wheat, "The Determinants of
1963–77 Regional Manufacturing Growth: When the South and West Grow," *Journal of Regional Science*, vol. 26 (November 1986), pp. 635–59. See Shelby Gerking
and William Morgan, "Measuring the Effects of Industrial Location and State Economic Development Policy: A Survey," in Herzog and Schlottmann, eds., *Industry
Location and Public Policy*, pp. 31–56, for a discussion of Wheat's methodology and
the methodology employed in more recent studies.

40. Thomas R. Plaut and Joseph E. Pluta, "Business Climate, Taxes, and Expenditures, and State Industrial Growth in the United States," *Southern Economic
Journal*, vol. 50 (July 1983), pp. 99–119; and Robert J. Newman, "Industry Migration
and Growth in the South," *Review of Economics and Statistics*, vol. 65 (February
1983), pp. 76–86.

41. Wheat does not include a wage variable in his analysis. Plaut and Pluta include both unionization and the wage rate, but the wage rate is statistically significant
in only one of three equations and then with a positive coefficient.

while Newman and Plaut and Pluta find that taxes are inversely related to state growth.

The more recent studies generally examine much narrower phenomena, such as the number of establishment starts in a few industries or direct foreign investment in selected manufacturing industries. These studies often use pooled time-series, cross-sectional analysis on panel data, such as census or Dun and Bradstreet data. The narrowness of their focus permits a much more precise estimation of the effects of industry-specific wage rates, state-specific subsidies, or industry tax rates on the level or rate of change in industrial activity. As Bartik points out, the later studies generally find a much more significant effect of state and local government tax or expenditure policies on growth than did the earlier more aggregative studies.[42] In fact, Bartik finds that 60 percent of recent studies contain at least one statistically significant public expenditures effect and 70 to 92 percent of the studies have at least one significant negative tax effect.

Many of the recent studies of regional growth are based on rather short time periods, some as few as two years. In contrast, my study utilizes a consistent framework to analyze the determinants of regional manufacturing growth during 1967–89 and even 1967–91 because I am interested in the persistence of divergent growth rates in manufacturing between the Rust Belt and the rest of the country. Unlike most of the recent studies, mine finds that tax, government expenditure, and infrastructure variables have not had consistent effects on manufacturing growth, although each has been associated with this growth in a significant way in some subperiod. For instance, the *TAX* variable is statistically significant during 1977–91 in the manufacturing employment growth equation but not during 1967–77. Infrastructure appears directly related to manufacturing employment growth in 1977–89, but not in 1967–77. Welfare expenditures are generally negatively related to overall nonfarm output and employment growth but not to manufacturing growth.

By contrast, labor market variables are consistently and negatively related to manufacturing growth over the entire period from 1967 to 1991, as are the regional dummy variables such as *ZONE*, *MOUNTAIN REGION*, and *NORTHTIER*. The long-run elasticities of manufacturing employment with respect to *UNION* and *WAGE*

42. Bartik, *Who Benefits*, pp. 17–62.

**Table 2-14. Coefficients of Important Variables in the Manufacturing Employment Growth Equations over Selected Periods, 1967–91**

| Variable[a] | 1967–77 | 1967–89 | 1967–91 |
|---|---|---|---|
| UNION (1966) | −0.74 | −1.34 | −1.43 |
| MOUNTAIN REGION | 0.104 | 0.235 | 0.197 |
| ZONE | 0.0290 | 0.0659 | 0.0752 |
| MARKET (1967) | 0.00186 | 0.00250 | 0.00287 |
| NORTHTIER | −0.135 | −0.436 | −0.396 |

a. Remaining variables in equation 2-6a are omitted from these regressions.

are relatively similar to the average elasticities calculated by Bartik from recent studies. Bartik reports that the average elasticities of business activity with respect to wages and unionization are −0.7 and −0.1, respectively.[43] My results over a twenty-four-year period translate into elasticities of −0.7 and −0.3, respectively, when each variable is entered separately.

Equally important is the fact that the labor market, regional dummy, and demand variable coefficients increase with the lag employed. Table 2-14 shows the coefficients of the five most important variables for 1967–77, 1967–89, and 1967–91. As expected, these coefficients grow at approximately a linear rate with the lag employed. This suggests that the formulation of persistent growth effects of these variables as specified in equation 2-6a is appropriate and that continued divergent growth can be expected unless the regional differences in some fundamental variable, such as wages or unionization, are reversed.

Finally, one might ask how the results would change if *current* values of the independent variables were substituted for the lagged, initial-period values in the manufacturing employment-growth equations.[44] Surprisingly, the results are virtually unchanged. In each period, *WAGE* and *UNION* assume negative coefficients when entered separately, and the negative coefficients of *UNION* are highly significant and of a very similar magnitude to those reported in table 2-5. The coefficients of *TAX* and *ENERGY* are generally not significantly different from zero.[45]

43. These are the "trimmed means" with controls for fixed effects as reported in Bartik, *Who Benefits*, tables 2.6, 2.7, pp. 51, 55.

44. Timothy Bartik has suggested to me that such a specification is more theoretically defensible. (Correspondence, March 22, 1993).

45. This consistency undoubtedly derives from the relative stability in the geographic distribution of the variables. See chapter 4.

*Chapter Three*

# Regional Changes in Income

---

MOST OF THE policy concern over the decline in manufacturing in the Rust Belt derives from its alleged impact on incomes in the North. As manufacturing leaves, workers are displaced
and forced to find other, potentially lower-paying jobs or to migrate
to other regions. The highest-wage jobs—in steel, automobiles, and
machinery—are the most likely to disappear, leaving behind an excess supply of industrial workers to compete against each other and
reduce the wages for the remaining jobs. Thus the common wisdom
is that blue-collar workers in the North suffer as industrial capital
moves to lower-wage states.

## Regional Shifts in Earned Incomes

How have earned incomes varied with the strength of manufacturing in each region? To answer this question, I analyzed the average income of full-time wage and salary earners in prime working
years responding to the Current Population Survey (CPS).[1]

Between 1967 and 1977, full-time workers in the northern census regions fared no worse than those in the rest of the country
despite the loss of 1 million manufacturing jobs in the period. Average real earned incomes rose by 9.5 to 13.9 percent in the North,
less than the 13.8 to 23.2 percent in the South but far more than the
3.8 to 9.3 percent in the two western regions (table 3-1).

1. Prime working years are defined as ages 20–54. Because of the limited size of
the CPS sample, I do not report the income averages by state. Rather, the weighted
averages are calculated by census region, using the weights provided by the CPS for
each demographic group in the survey. These weighted averages are then stated in
1982 dollars, using the implicit personal consumption expenditure deflator. Separate
regional deflators for personal consumption outlays are not available.

**Table 3-1. Average Annual Earned Real Income for Full-Time Workers, Aged 20–54, Selected Years, 1967–89**[a]

Income in 1982 dollars

| Region | 1967 | 1977 | 1989 | Percent change 1967–77 | Percent change 1977–89 |
|---|---|---|---|---|---|
| | | | *All workers* | | |
| New England | 20,627 | 22,579 | 25,988 | 9.5 | 15.1 |
| Middle Atlantic | 21,280 | 24,032 | 25,120 | 12.9 | 4.5 |
| East north central | 21,337 | 24,301 | 23,535 | 13.9 | −3.2 |
| West north central | 20,521 | 22,246 | 21,166 | 8.4 | −4.9 |
| South Atlantic | 18,827 | 21,430 | 21,494 | 13.8 | 0.3 |
| East south central | 16,641 | 20,495 | 19,379 | 23.2 | 5.4 |
| West south central | 18,282 | 21,725 | 20,930 | 18.8 | −3.7 |
| Mountain | 20,343 | 22,225 | 21,217 | 9.3 | −4.5 |
| Pacific | 23,306 | 24,185 | 24,148 | 3.8 | −0.2 |
| U.S. average | 20,562 | 22,956 | 22,292 | 11.6 | −0.7 |
| | | | *Workers in manufacturing sector* | | |
| New England | 20,831 | 22,255 | 27,426 | 6.8 | 23.2 |
| Middle Atlantic | 21,469 | 24,739 | 25,589 | 15.2 | 3.4 |
| East north central | 21,612 | 25,522 | 24,547 | 18.1 | −3.8 |
| West north central | 21,605 | 23,371 | 22,458 | 8.2 | −3.9 |
| South Atlantic | 18,501 | 21,195 | 21,387 | 14.6 | 0.9 |
| East south central | 16,828 | 20,311 | 19,666 | 20.7 | −3.2 |
| West south central | 19,506 | 22,768 | 23,248 | 16.7 | 2.1 |
| Mountain | 21,432 | 23,827 | 22,847 | 11.2 | −4.1 |
| Pacific | 24,248 | 24,652 | 25,114 | 1.7 | 1.9 |
| U.S. average | 21,065 | 23,734 | 23,780 | 12.7 | 0.2 |

Source: Current Population Survey (March 1968, 1978, 1990), machine-readable data file (Bureau of the Census, 1968, 1978, 1990).

a. Deflated by the personal consumption expenditure deflator.

After 1977, average real earned incomes fell for the two north central regions, but real income growth in the Northeast was substantially above the stagnant national average of −0.7 percent for 1977–89. Real earned incomes grew much more rapidly in New England and the middle Atlantic region than in the South even though manufacturing employment trends exhibited the reverse pattern—a continued decline in New England and the middle Atlantic states and a steady expansion in all the southern regions. Moreover, there was no growth in real earned incomes in the mountain and Pacific regions despite the very rapid western growth in manufacturing in 1977–89.

In short, there is very little evidence that the shift in manufacturing employment since 1967 has been reflected in changes in the regional distribution of average earned incomes for full-time workers. Over the 1967–77 period, there is a mild but statistically insignificant direct correlation between real income growth and manufacturing employment growth across the regions. Between 1977 and 1989, there is an *inverse* but statistically insignificant correlation between these two growth rates.

Nor are the conclusions different for the distribution of real income gains for manufacturing workers. The bottom panel of table 3-1 provides the same data for workers employed full time in manufacturing. Again, workers in the east north central and middle Atlantic regions do not generally suffer relative to their counterparts in the South and West despite the disparate growth rates in manufacturing employment. Western manufacturing workers' incomes grew substantially less rapidly than the U.S. average in both periods, and southern workers' incomes grew only marginally more rapidly after 1977. As in the larger sample, the New England and middle Atlantic states evidenced more rapid income growth despite the steep decline in manufacturing employment in both regions.

Why have regional earnings not reflected the shift in manufacturing employment? One part of the answer is that manufacturing employment is a small share of total employment in every region, and some of the other sectors—such as construction—have filled the employment void left by the disappearing manufacturing base in northern regions. Another part of the answer may be found in the regional structure of manufacturing wages. Despite the dramatic shifts in manufacturing, the regional structure of manufacturing wages has changed very little since 1967 (table 3-2). Southern manufacturing wages have risen by about 4 percent relative to the U.S. average, but they remain below the national average. Western wages have fallen by about 8 percent relative to the national average despite the strong growth in manufacturing employment in western states, and northern wages, except in New England, show virtually no change in their share of the national average. Given this remarkable regional stability in manufacturing wages and the growth in nonmanufacturing sectors, it is not surprising that the shift in manufacturing employment has not been associated with a major shift in the regional distribution of earnings.

**Table 3-2. Hourly Earnings in Manufacturing, by Region, Selected Years, 1967–89**

Earnings in dollars per hour

|  | 1967 | | 1977 | | 1989 | |
|---|---|---|---|---|---|---|
| Region | Earnings | Share of U.S. average | Earnings | Share of U.S. average | Earnings | Share of U.S. average |
| New England | 2.68 | 0.95 | 5.09 | 0.90 | 10.65 | 1.02 |
| Middle Atlantic | 2.87 | 1.02 | 5.77 | 1.02 | 10.78 | 1.03 |
| East north central | 3.19 | 1.13 | 6.72 | 1.18 | 12.02 | 1.15 |
| West north central | 2.89 | 1.02 | 5.83 | 1.03 | 10.57 | 1.01 |
| South Atlantic | 2.31 | 0.82 | 4.63 | 0.82 | 9.08 | 0.87 |
| East south central | 2.36 | 0.84 | 4.85 | 0.85 | 9.22 | 0.88 |
| West south central | 2.59 | 0.92 | 5.29 | 0.93 | 10.07 | 0.96 |
| Mountain | 2.94 | 1.04 | 5.60 | 0.99 | 10.13 | 0.97 |
| Pacific | 3.28 | 1.16 | 6.17 | 1.09 | 11.26 | 1.07 |
| U.S. average | 2.82 | . . . | 5.68 | . . . | 10.49 | . . . |

Source: Author's calculations based on data from *Employment and Earnings*, May issues (1968, 1978, 1979, 1990).

## Major Demographic Groups

It is possible that the above results reflect a shift in the composition of the labor force and that the changes in industrial structure have had measurable effects on the demographic groups most likely to be employed in manufacturing. To test for this possibility, I examined the growth in real earned incomes for just those workers aged 20–54 with twelve to fifteen years of education, that is, those who completed high school but not college. It is from this group that manufacturing production workers are most likely to be drawn. In addition, I divided full-time workers with twelve to fifteen years of education into four separate demographic groups: white males, black males, white females, and black females.

The average incomes for each of these four demographic groups in each of the nine census regions are displayed in table 3-3. Note that the increases in average real income for the entire country over 1967–77 are smallest for white males. Black males do better, and black and white females decidedly outgain their male counterparts. In the 1977–89 period, black and white males suffer similar declines in real income, but females' income continues to rise—albeit at a slower rate. These results are consistent with other research on

**Table 3-3. Average Annual Earned Real Income for Full-Time Workers with 12–15 Years of Education, by Race and Sex, Selected Years, 1967–89**
Income in 1982 dollars

| | | | | Percent change | |
|---|---|---|---|---|---|
| *Region* | *1967* | *1977* | *1989* | *1967–77* | *1977–89* |
| | | | *White males* | | |
| New England | 20,834 | 22,012 | 24,524 | 5.7 | 11.4 |
| Middle Atlantic | 22,638 | 24,359 | 24,150 | 7.6 | −0.9 |
| East north central | 22,647 | 25,011 | 23,486 | 10.4 | −6.1 |
| West north central | 20,887 | 22,316 | 20,326 | 6.8 | −8.9 |
| South Atlantic | 20,832 | 22,403 | 21,498 | 7.5 | −4.0 |
| East south central | 19,368 | 22,882 | 20,822 | 8.1 | −9.0 |
| West south central | 20,234 | 22,921 | 21,000 | 13.3 | −8.4 |
| Mountain | 20,681 | 22,709 | 20,593 | 9.8 | −9.3 |
| Pacific | 23,672 | 25,214 | 23,797 | 6.5 | −3.6 |
| U.S. average | 21,891 | 23,731 | 22,527 | 6.8 | −3.6 |
| | | | *Black males* | | |
| New England | 18,548 | 20,830 | 18,676 | 12.3 | −10.3 |
| Middle Atlantic | 16,135 | 19,789 | 21,226 | 22.6 | 7.3 |
| East north central | 16,974 | 22,315 | 20,677 | 31.5 | −7.3 |
| West north central | 16,031 | 15,641 | 16,942 | −2.4 | 8.3 |
| South Atlantic | 13,405 | 17,118 | 16,021 | 27.7 | −6.4 |
| East south central | 11,278 | 14,703 | 15,385 | 30.4 | 4.6 |
| West south central | 12,554 | 16,616 | 16,141 | 32.4 | −2.9 |
| Mountain | 17,462 | 20,506 | 16,043 | 17.4 | −21.8 |
| Pacific | 17,720 | 20,585 | 21,152 | 16.2 | 2.8 |
| U.S. average | 15,528 | 18,748 | 18,482 | 20.7 | −4.4 |
| | | | *White females* | | |
| New England | 12,192 | 14,489 | 17,026 | 18.8 | 17.5 |
| Middle Atlantic | 13,283 | 15,294 | 15,897 | 15.1 | 3.9 |
| East north central | 12,709 | 14,592 | 14,924 | 14.8 | 2.3 |
| West north central | 12,093 | 13,096 | 14,078 | 8.3 | 7.5 |
| South Atlantic | 11,957 | 13,557 | 14,605 | 13.4 | 7.7 |
| East south central | 11,322 | 13,626 | 12,409 | 20.3 | −8.9 |
| West south central | 11,399 | 13,453 | 14,601 | 18.0 | 8.5 |
| Mountain | 12,740 | 13,636 | 14,418 | 7.0 | 5.7 |
| Pacific | 13,660 | 15,307 | 17,551 | 12.1 | 14.7 |
| U.S. average | 12,643 | 14,365 | 15,267 | 13.6 | 6.3 |

**Table 3-3** *Continued*

| Region | 1967 | 1977 | 1989 | Percent change 1967–77 | Percent change 1977–89 |
|---|---|---|---|---|---|
| | | | *Black females* | | |
| New England | a | a | 13,465 | ... | ... |
| Middle Atlantic | 10,804 | 14,233 | 15,784 | 31.7 | 10.9 |
| East north central | 11,380 | 15,297 | 16,011 | 34.4 | 4.7 |
| West north central | a | 11,018 | 11,194 | −0.4 | 1.6 |
| South Atlantic | 9,035 | 12,609 | 14,000 | 39.6 | 11.6 |
| East south central | a | 10,288 | 12,067 | ... | 17.3 |
| West south central | 8,724 | 12,235 | 11,341 | 40.2 | −7.3 |
| Mountain | a | a | 13,060 | ... | ... |
| Pacific | 11,325 | 13,786 | 16,986 | 21.7 | 23.2 |
| U.S. average | 10,102 | 13,510 | 14,225 | 33.7 | 5.3 |

Source: CPS (March 1968, 1978, 1990), machine-readable data file.
a. Small sample (fewer than ten observations).

the narrowing race and gender differentials in the United States,[2] but they also shed some light on why there is so much concern over the declining prospects for relatively uneducated blue-collar labor.[3] In particular, white males with only a high school education have shown very little improvement in real living standards since 1967, and black males' real incomes have stagnated since 1977. However, the sharp deceleration in income growth since 1977 for all four demographic groups cannot be readily attributed to the relative decline in manufacturing employment, which began long before 1977.

As in the case of the average earned income for all demographic groups (shown in table 3-1), there appears to be no correlation between regional changes in manufacturing and the change in real earnings for any of the groups with twelve to fifteen years of education (table 3-3). In 1967–77, all groups did better in the South than in the North, but those in the West did not fare well. After 1977, black and white males generally exhibited negative real income growth in the South and West, but their results in New England and the middle Atlantic states were mixed. White females' real income gains continued at a somewhat slower rate in most regions, but black females experienced a sharp deceleration in all regions except the Pacific. Whatever the causes of these disparate

2. James P. Smith and Finis R. Welch, *Closing the Gap: Forty Years of Economic Progress for Blacks* (Santa Monica: Rand Corporation, February 1986).

3. Frank Levy, *Dollars and Dreams: The Changing American Income Distribution* (New York: Russell Sage Foundation, 1987), chap. 7.

movements in real earnings, it is unlikely that they were related to the shift in manufacturing to the South and West.

## Regional Wage Premiums

To correct more explicitly for demographic changes in the labor force, I utilize the Current Population Survey data to fit a human-capital equation of the standard variety:[4]

$$(3\text{-}1)\ \text{Log}\ Y = a_0 + a_1\ EDUC + a_2\ EDUC^{**}2 + a_3\ EDUC^*EXPER$$
$$+ a_4\ EXPER + a_5\ EXPER^{**}2 + a_6\ SEX$$
$$+ a_7\ WHITE + a_8\ BLACK + u,$$

where *EDUC* is years of education completed, *EXPER* is estimated years of labor force experience, *SEX* is a dummy variable equal to unity if the worker is male and zero otherwise, *WHITE* is a dummy variable equal to unity if the worker is white and zero otherwise, and *BLACK* is a dummy variable equal to unity if the worker is black and zero otherwise. Estimates of this equation were obtained for all full-time workers in 1967, 1977, and 1989, and the residuals from the equation are a measure of how much higher average regional earnings were in current dollars than predicted by the national relationship between similar demographic characteristics and earned income.

The changes in these average residuals for each region between 1967 and 1989 and between 1977 and 1989 are shown in table 3-4. In general, the two northeastern census regions appear to have improved their relative earning power while most other regions showed a decline. There is an *inverse* but statistically insignificant correlation between these residuals and the growth in total nonfarm or manufacturing employment between the relevant years. Hence the earning power of full-time workers does not appear to be related to the overall rate of growth of manufacturing or total employment.

The average residuals for each state offer a more precise analysis. A regression of the change in these residuals on the changes in nonfarm employment, manufacturing employment, and the unemploy-

4. See Robert J. Willis, "Wage Determinants: A Survey and Reinterpretation of Human Capital Earnings Functions," in Orley Ashenfelter and Richard Layard, eds., *Handbook of Labor Economics*, vol. 1 (New York: North Holland Press, 1986), pp. 525–602.

**Table 3-4. Change in Annual Earnings, Adjusted for Human Capital, Selected Periods, 1967–89**

Percent

| Region | 1967–89 | 1977–89 |
|---|---|---|
| New England | 8.6 | 13.4 |
| Middle Atlantic | 4.0 | 4.9 |
| East north central | −2.2 | −3.2 |
| West north central | −9.4 | −6.4 |
| South Atlantic | 1.2 | −1.3 |
| East south central | 7.5 | −0.1 |
| West south central | −1.4 | −3.8 |
| Mountain | −7.2 | −5.1 |
| Pacific | −4.5 | −2.2 |

Source: CPS (March 1968, 1978, 1990), machine-readable data file.

ment rate results in negative and significant coefficients for changes in the unemployment rate and changes in manufacturing employment. This suggests that the tightness in the overall labor market is directly correlated with the excess earnings rate, but that changes in excess earnings are inversely related with the growth in manufacturing employment. The latter result must indicate that manufacturing industries have been moving to areas with falling excess earning levels, not that earnings are depressed by the growth of manufacturing.

## Effect on Black Workers

The results in table 3-3 suggest that black male workers with a high school education fared no worse than their white counterparts after 1977 in most regions and that their incomes rose more rapidly than white males' between 1967 and 1977 in every census region (except the west north central region, in which there are very few black workers). Recently, however, John Bound and Richard Freeman have found that the decline of Rust Belt manufacturing has substantially harmed young black male workers in these regions.[5] Their result is confined to northeastern and midwestern black males with a high school education or less and fewer than ten years of

5. John Bound and Richard B. Freeman, "What Went Wrong? The Erosion of Relative Earnings and Employment among Young Black Men in the 1980s," Working Paper 3778 (Cambridge, Mass.: National Bureau of Economic Research, June 1991).

**Table 3-5. Male Full-Time Workers in Durable-Goods Manufacturing, Middle Atlantic and East North Central Regions, by Race and Experience, Selected Years, 1967–89**

Percent

| Race and experience | 1967 | 1977 | 1989 |
|---|---|---|---|
| All full-time black male workers | 30.8 | 28.9 | 19.4 |
| Black workers with less than 10 years' experience | 36.0 | 25.4 | 13.5 |
| Black workers with 10 or more years' experience | 30.1 | 29.4 | 20.3 |
| All full-time workers (all races) | 34.7 | 28.0 | 20.1 |

Source: CPS (March 1968, 1978, 1990), machine-readable data file.

work experience. This subset of the population is so small that shifts in its fortunes are unlikely to have affected the real-income trends shown in table 3-3. For example, in the March 1967 CPS sample, this category of workers accounts for only 1.0 percent of the nation's full-time workers and only 11.1 percent of all black male full-time workers.[6] Moreover, only about one-third of all black male full-time workers were employed in manufacturing in 1967. Nevertheless, the loss of manufacturing jobs could have severe effects on young new black male entrants to the labor force, surely a high-risk group in the United States.

Have young black male workers tended to be overrepresented in manufacturing in the Rust Belt states? If so, the decline of manufacturing might have affected them more than other demographic groups. Table 3-5, drawn from the March CPS data, shows that in 1967, 36 percent of young black full-time male workers in these states were employed in manufacturing, about the same as the overall share of manufacturing employment in total nonfarm employment in these states. By 1989, however, the young black male share had fallen to 13.5 percent, far below the average for all workers in the Rust Belt. At the same time, older black workers in the Rust Belt were much more successful in retaining their share of manufacturing jobs in this region.

These results lead to the unsurprising conclusion that the shift of

6. Bound and Freeman use a different CPS file—the "usual weekly data file"—for their analysis because it has three times as many observations as the March CPS that I use in this analysis. Unfortunately, the usual weekly file is available only from 1979 on.

**Table 3-6. Durable-Goods Manufacturing Wage Premiums over Lowest-Paid Sector for Full-Time Male Workers, by Race, Selected Years, 1967–89**
Percent

| Race and region | 1967 | 1977 | 1989 |
|---|---|---|---|
| *Entire country* | | | |
| Nonblack | 16.2 | 23.7 | 23.5 |
| Black | 31.6 | 28.3 | 27.6 |
| *Rust Belt* | | | |
| Nonblack | 18.2 | 23.3 | 21.2 |
| Black | 32.9 | 37.4[a] | 23.7[a] |

Source: CPS (March 1968, 1978, 1990), machine-readable data file.
a. Not statistically significant.

manufacturing out of the Rust Belt has not had much impact on existing job holders, such as black males; rather, it has sharply reduced the access to manufacturing jobs for new entrants into the labor force. Because manufacturing jobs pay higher wages than other employment, perhaps in part because of unionization, the loss of these early opportunities may be quite serious.

The size of the wage premium in manufacturing may be deduced from estimating the human-capital equation (3-1) with the addition of dummy variables for each major industry.[7] I estimated these equations for black and nonblack male workers in the entire country and in the Rust Belt. Rather than report the detailed results, I show the size of the premium for durable-goods manufacturing over the lowest-paid sector for each group in each geographical grouping for 1967, 1977, and 1989 (see table 3-6). These results clearly show that black male workers in manufacturing enjoy far larger premiums than other male workers in manufacturing, although the results for the Rust Belt are clouded by lack of statistical significance in 1977 and 1989. Surprisingly, the nonblack male manufacturing premium actually *rose* over the period, although it is still below the premium for black male workers. Once again, this suggests that the major regional shifts in manufacturing have not eroded manufacturing wages relative to other wages in the economy.

It is possible to estimate the effect of the shift in the mix of industry on black workers since 1967. Assume that black male workers retained their 1967 industry mix and enjoyed the continuation

7. Separate dummy variables are included for services, durable manufacturing, nondurable manufacturing, wholesale and retail trade, transportation and public utilities, finance, insurance, and real estate, mining, and construction.

of the 1967 wage premiums in durable-goods manufacturing. Under this scenario, the average black male's annual earnings from full-time employment would have been 2.3 percent higher in 1989 than the earnings he actually received, but young, inexperienced black males would have earned 6.7 percent more. Thus the lack of entry opportunities into manufacturing appears to have had a significant effect on the annual earnings of young black males but a much more modest effect on older black workers. If young black entrants into the labor force have been displaced into part-time work by the shift in industrial structure, the effects may have been even greater. Part-time employment has indeed risen over the past two decades, but it is difficult to estimate the causes of that shift.

# Chapter Four

# Will the Regional Shift in Manufacturing Continue?

AS I HAVE shown, there has been no sharp rebound in Rust Belt manufacturing since 1985 despite a sharp decline in the value of the dollar and a continuing decline in real energy prices. Indeed, by 1991 the middle Atlantic states' share of U.S. manufacturing employment was fully 2 percentage points below its 1985 share of 16 percent. The other group of states in the Rust Belt, the east north central census region, showed only a 0.2 percent increase in its share of the country's manufacturing jobs in the same period, hardly a robust turnaround. I now return to the results of the equations in chapter 2 to explain the continuing regional migration of manufacturing.

## Forecasting the 1977–89 and 1985–89 Periods

Whatever the causes of the Rust Belt's continuing decline in manufacturing, one might think that it would have been arrested by a narrowing of the regional differences in the underlying microeconomic determinants of location, such as wages, unionization, resource prices, or tax rates. Before turning to this question, however, it is useful to see if recent growth rates differ markedly from those that would have been predicted from the reduced-form equations of employment growth from earlier periods. For this purpose, I utilize equations of the form reflected in table 2-5, estimated for 1967–77 and for 1967–85, to forecast employment growth for 1977–89 and 1985–89.[1]

---

1. Specifically, I include only those variables whose coefficients are statistically significant. These include *UNION, WAGE, ZONE, MARKET, MOUNTAIN RE-GION, NORTHTIER*, and *ENERGY* (in the later regression). These variables explain

**Table 4-1. Difference between Real and Predicted Annual Rate of Change in Manufacturing Employment, 1977–89 and 1985–89**
Percent

| Region | Forecast period (1977–89) and regression period (1967–77) | Forecast period (1985–89) and regression period (1967–85) |
|---|---|---|
| New England | −0.5 | −2.0 |
| Middle Atlantic | −0.3 | −0.3 |
| East north central | −0.5 | 1.3 |
| West north central | −1.0 | 1.3 |
| South Atlantic | −0.5 | 0.2 |
| East south central | −1.0 | 1.2 |
| West south central | −2.0 | −1.1 |
| Mountain | −2.2 | −1.4 |
| Pacific | −0.6 | 0.8 |
| Average U.S. state | −1.0 | −0.1 |

Source: Author's calculations.

The forecast errors for 1977–89 and 1985–89 were obtained for each of the lower forty-eight states and regressed on dummy variables for each census region to obtain the average (unweighted) value for each region. These errors are shown in table 4-1 with the average error for all forty-eight states. Note that both equations systematically overpredict manufacturing employment growth, by 1 percent a year in 1977–89 and by 0.1 percent a year in 1985–89.

More important for present purposes, table 4-1 shows that the Rust Belt regions marginally outperformed the U.S. average, given the changes in underlying variables between 1967 and 1977. After 1985 the east north central states fared much better than the average region relative to predictions, but the middle Atlantic states exhibited a decline relative to the predictions. In the more recent period, the southern and western regions generally outperformed the rest of the country once again.

## Shifts in the Underlying Variables

The continuing shift of manufacturing away from the traditional northern regions might be expected to place downward pressure on

approximately 80 percent of the variance in employment growth in the two respective periods.

the price of resources—particularly labor—in the North and upward pressure on these prices in the Sun Belt. Such an adjustment would serve to slow if not stop the migration, establishing a new equilibrium in the regional distribution of industry. On the other hand, if population migration is sufficiently great for other reasons—such as climate—there might be little change in the regional distribution of wages.

### Labor Market Variables

In the empirical analysis reported above, wage rates (or the rental price of human capital), unionization, distance from the Rust Belt, and a proxy for demand appear to have the greatest effects on the rate of change in manufacturing jobs. Taxes, energy prices, state and local spending, and infrastructure generally have less systematic effects. Nevertheless, in this section I show how all of these variables changed in 1967–89.

The results in chapter 3 suggested that the migration of industry had little apparent impact on earned incomes for full-time employees during 1967–89. The data shown in table 4-2 buttress this finding. Average manufacturing wages actually exhibit a slight widening of the differential between the Rust Belt and the rest of the country. These wage rates, however, are not corrected for changes in relative human capital.

Table 4-2 also shows excess earned income—the average percentage errors from a human-capital equation for all full-time workers aged 25–54 captured by the CPS (my *WAGE* variable in the regression analysis). Once again, the gap between regions appears to have widened between 1967 and 1977. Between 1977 and 1989, the gap narrowed, in large part because of the growth in incomes in New England. Thus the migration of industry to the South and West is not closing the wage gap between the regions.

The rate of unionization by state is not available as a consistent, continuous series for 1967–89; however, data for all nonfarm employment are available from the BLS for 1966–78, and unionization estimates for manufacturing are available from the Grant Thornton *Manufacturing Climates Studies* for 1984–89 (table 4-3). Both series exhibit the same general pattern of decline, but the *rate* of decline is greater for the other states than for Rust Belt states. As a result,

**Table 4-2. Trends in Wages and Earnings by Region, Selected Years, 1967–89**

| Region | Manufacturing wage (dollars per hour) | | | Excess earned income, full-time workers (percent) | | |
|---|---|---|---|---|---|---|
| | 1967 | 1977 | 1989 | 1967 | 1977 | 1989 |
| New England | 2.68 | 5.09 | 10.65 | −1.5 | −6.3 | 7.1 |
| Middle Atlantic | 2.87 | 5.77 | 10.78 | 4.3 | 3.4 | 8.3 |
| East north central | 3.19 | 6.72 | 12.02 | 6.6 | 7.6 | 4.4 |
| West north central | 2.89 | 5.83 | 10.57 | −4.4 | −7.4 | −13.8 |
| South Atlantic | 2.31 | 4.63 | 9.08 | −6.9 | −4.4 | −5.7 |
| East south central | 2.36 | 4.85 | 9.22 | −17.5 | −9.9 | −10.0 |
| West south central | 2.59 | 5.29 | 10.07 | −9.8 | −7.4 | −11.2 |
| Mountain | 2.94 | 5.60 | 10.13 | −4.0 | −6.1 | −11.2 |
| Pacific | 3.28 | 6.17 | 11.26 | 8.9 | 6.6 | 4.4 |
| Rust Belt | 3.04 | 6.32 | 11.52 | 5.5 | 6.4 | 5.7 |
| Rest of country | 2.70 | 5.29 | 10.11 | −3.7 | −3.8 | −4.9 |

Sources: Department of Labor, Bureau of Labor Statistics, Current Employment Statistics, State and Area Industry Employment data.

the gap between the two regions of the country in relative unionization appears to have widened slightly.

The wage rate and unionization trends are consistent with another general result. In each of the three years for which I have estimated excess earnings rates, the level of excess earnings is directly correlated with the rate of unionization. Therefore it is not surprising that there has been a slight widening of the earnings gap between the two regions in the past two decades.

The expansion of the gap between the average Rust Belt wage and the average wage in the rest of the country may appear to contradict the general finding of wage convergence in the United States reported in chapter 2. But wages may indeed converge on average across all states while diverging slightly between the eight Rust Belt states and the rest of the country.

The convergence in wages may be impeded somewhat by structural conditions in the labor market. For example, a simple wage convergence equation fitted to 1967–89 wage growth provides the following results when estimated over fifty states (*t*-statistics are shown in parentheses):

$$(4\text{-}1) \quad Log(WAGE89/WAGE67)/22 = 0.08 - 0.08\ LogWAGE67.$$
$$(6.24)$$

$$\bar{R}^2 = 0.436$$

**Table 4-3. Unionization Trends, by Region, Selected Years, 1966–89**
Percent of employment

| | Nonfarm employment | | Manufacturing | |
|---|---|---|---|---|
| Region | 1966 | 1978 | 1984 | 1989 |
| New England | 25.0 | 22.5 | 16.8 | 16.1 |
| Middle Atlantic | 36.3 | 34.4 | 40.5 | 39.2 |
| East north central | 36.2 | 31.0 | 42.5 | 37.6 |
| West north central | 27.2 | 21.9 | 22.0 | 19.4 |
| South Atlantic | 15.3 | 13.4 | 11.3 | 10.0 |
| East south central | 19.9 | 18.4 | 17.9 | 14.1 |
| West south central | 17.9 | 12.5 | 16.3 | 14.3 |
| Mountain | 20.9 | 15.4 | 9.7 | 7.2 |
| Pacific | 32.7 | 25.1 | 26.3 | 22.8 |
| Rust Belt | 36.2 | 32.5 | 41.6 | 38.3 |
| Rest of country | 22.2 | 18.2 | 17.7 | 15.5 |

Sources: Department of Labor, Bureau of Labor Statistics, *Directory of National and International Labor Unions in the United States, 1969*, bulletin 1665 (1970), p. 76; Department of Labor, Bureau of Labor Statistics, *Handbook of Labor Statistics*, bulletin 2070 (December 1980); *10th Annual Grant Thornton Manufacturing Climates Study* (Chicago: Grant Thornton, June 1989); and *11th Annual Grant Thornton Manufacturing Climates Study* (Chicago: Grant Thornton, August 1990).

If the degree of unionization tends to slow convergence by keeping wages high in heavily unionized states, this effect should be evident when the unionization variable is added to equation (4–1). The resulting estimate is:

(4-1a)    $\text{Log}(WAGE89/WAGE67)/22 = 0.08$
$$- 0.26 \, \text{Log}WAGE67 + 0.019 \, UNION.$$
$$\quad\quad (7.19) \quad\quad\quad\quad (3.26)$$
$$\bar{R}^2 = 0.530$$

Given wage rates and unionization in the two regions in 1966–67, equation 4-1a predicts the Rust Belt's nominal annual wage growth to be only 0.2 percent lower than the wage growth in the rest of the country over the 1967–89 period. Had the unionization rate been the same across the country—28 percent of the nonfarm work force in 1966—the rate of convergence would have been much faster: Rust Belt wage growth would have been 0.65 percent a year slower than wage growth in the rest of the country. Thus unionization appears to have placed a major drag on wage convergence between the Rust Belt and the South or West.

**Table 4-4. Total State and Local Expenditures per Capita, Selected Years, 1967–87**

Current dollars

| Region | 1967 | 1977 | 1987 |
|---|---|---|---|
| New England | 464 | 1,270 | 2,840 |
| Middle Atlantic | 507 | 1,505 | 3,227 |
| East north central | 439 | 1,217 | 2,568 |
| West north central | 469 | 1,187 | 2,581 |
| South Atlantic | 396 | 1,125 | 2,396 |
| East south central | 383 | 1,003 | 2,071 |
| West south central | 411 | 1,034 | 2,301 |
| Mountain | 543 | 1,281 | 2,775 |
| Pacific | 632 | 1,499 | 3,097 |
| Rust Belt | 472 | 1,354 | 2,879 |
| Rest of country | 471 | 1,210 | 2,591 |

Source: Bureau of the Census, *1982 Census of Governments*, vol. 6, no. 4: "Historical Statistics on Governmental Finances and Employment" (Department of Commerce, January 1985), table 24.

## Taxes and Government Spending

As with the labor market variables, the difference in tax rates between the two regions has shifted against the Rust Belt since 1967. Total state tax collections in Rust Belt states rose from 9.6 percent of state personal income in 1967 to 11.7 percent in 1987 while rising only from 10.0 percent to 10.7 percent in the rest of the country. Similarly, corporate tax collections in Rust Belt states rose from 1.2 percent of manufacturing incomes in 1967 to 3.5 percent in 1987 while rising only from 2.1 percent to 3.9 percent in the rest of the country over the same period.[2]

In light of the tax collection trends, it is not surprising that per capita state and local government expenditures also show a sharper rise for Rust Belt states than for the rest of the country over 1967–87 (table 4-4). In particular, western states show a substantially lower rate of increase in per capita government expenditures than do the Rust Belt states—and western states' manufacturing sectors grew rapidly after 1977. Whether these increases in spending are the cause or the effect of the shift in manufacturing is debatable, but other studies suggest that rising relative government expenditures are as likely to reduce business activity as to increase it.[3]

2. Data are from Bureau of the Census and Department of Commerce, Bureau of Economic Analysis.

3. Timothy J. Bartik, *Who Benefits from State and Local Economic Development Policies?* (Kalamazoo: W. E. Upjohn Institute for Employment Research, 1991) table

**Table 4-5.  Real Infrastructure per Capita, 1970 and 1987[a]**

1982 dollars

| Region | 1970 | 1987 |
|--------|------|------|
| New England | 4,349 | 5,128 |
| Middle Atlantic | 4,888 | 6,169 |
| East north central | 4,703 | 5,319 |
| West north central | 5,186 | 6,452 |
| South Atlantic | 4,015 | 5,028 |
| East south central | 4,832 | 5,232 |
| West south central | 4,749 | 5,405 |
| Mountain | 5,962 | 6,631 |
| Pacific | 6,220 | 5,740 |
| Rust Belt | 4,792 | 5,720 |
| Rest of country | 5,061 | 5,557 |

Sources: Alicia H. Munnell, "How Does Public Infrastructure Affect Regional Economic Performance?" *New England Economic Review* (September–October 1990), pp. 11–32.

a. Infrastructure defined as highways and streets; water and sewer systems; government buildings, other structures, and equipment.

Finally, despite much of the recent concern about state infrastructure and growth, the Rust Belt states show not only higher levels of infrastructure per capita in 1987 than the rest of the country, but also a higher rate of increase (table 4-5). Even though there is only limited evidence that a state's infrastructure matters much in manufacturing employment or output growth, clearly the recent trends in infrastructure growth are not the cause of the Rust Belt's declining manufacturing base.

## Stopping the Migration

If wages, unionization, taxes, or government spending are indeed contributors to the Rust Belt's decline, there is nothing in their trends that would suggest a cessation of the westward and southern migration of manufacturing. Indeed, the results in chapter 2 suggest that distance from the Rust Belt (the *ZONE* variable) and mountain region location were at least as powerful in explaining the shift of manufacturing jobs in 1977–89 as in 1967–77. It appears that a southern or western location would have continued to

---

2.5. Bartik finds that the proportion of studies that have at least one statistically significant *positive* public expenditure variable coefficient is about the same as the proportion of studies with one statistically significant *negative* welfare variable coefficient.

generate more manufacturing job growth even if wages, unionization rates, and (less important) taxes had equalized across the regions.

As manufacturing continues to shift away from the Rust Belt, of course, the industries that remain may be those that find that the Rust Belt offers locational advantages over the South and West. Thus future analyses may find a natural slowing of the migration that my 1967–89 analysis did not uncover. By the peak of the last business cycle, however, such decelerating forces had not appeared in the middle Atlantic states, although they may be arising in the Great Lakes states. It is therefore perhaps of some interest to ask what changes in the underlying microeconomic variables would have been required to stabilize the regional distribution of manufacturing at earlier levels. The two obvious choices for such an analysis are wages and taxes.

As I have shown, the results in chapter 2 and the central tendency of a large body of previous studies suggest an elasticity of employment or output with respect to wages of $-0.7$.[4] And although my analysis did not uncover a systematic effect of state and local taxes on state activity, Bartik's summary of earlier studies finds a mean estimate of about $-0.3$.[5]

Assume that the total size of the U.S. manufacturing sector would not be affected by any changes in Rust Belt conditions. In other words, lower Rust Belt wages or taxes would slow the migration of employment to other regions in the United States but not to other regions of the world. How much lower would Rust Belt wages or taxes had to have been in 1967 or 1977 in order to generate manufacturing employment growth equal to the national average in 1967–77 or 1977–89? Under these assumptions, the declines would have had to be sizable. Wages would had to have been 14 percent lower in 1967 or 24 percent lower in 1977 to hold the Rust Belt's share of manufacturing employment in the ensuing period, ceteris paribus. Alternatively, taxes in the Rust Belt region would had to have been 30.3 and 47 percent lower, respectively, in 1967 and 1977 to stabilize the area's share of manufacturing jobs. Had both taxes and wages been lowered, the reductions could obviously have been somewhat lower.

4. Bartik, table 2.6.
5. Bartik, table 2.3. The range of "trimmed mean" elasticities for interarea studies is $-0.22$ to $-0.43$.

These estimates of the magnitude of wage or tax concessions necessary to stabilize post-1967 Rust Belt manufacturing are probably too high. If wages or taxes were to decline, the Rust Belt would become more competitive with Canada or other countries at given exchange rates. But given the trends in Rust Belt wages and tax rates, even one-half or less of these estimated reductions seem unattainable over any reasonable future horizon. Thus, if the locational advantages of western or southern states that emerged from the statistical analysis of chapter 2 remain, it is very unlikely that the Rust Belt's share of manufacturing can stabilize at even its current levels despite the stability in the Great Lakes states since 1985.

## Conclusion

Whatever the cause of the migration of manufacturing from the Rust Belt—wages, unionization, state and local taxes, or government spending—there is little reason to hope that this migration will abate in the next few years or even decades. The differences in wages, unionization, tax collections, and government spending between the Rust Belt and the rest of the country have shown no signs of narrowing in the past quarter century. Moreover, even if these differences were to narrow somewhat, the natural advantages of the South and West would continue to attract manufacturing away from the colder, apparently less desirable sections of the country. This is not to say that government policies could not slow the migration of industry, but it is extremely unlikely that any set of policies can fully offset the disadvantages of the North in attracting new manufacturing activity.

*Chapter Five*

# The Core Industries of Rust Belt Manufacturing

THE EMPIRICAL ANALYSIS thus far has been rather general and somewhat abstract. To provide more of a real world context to these results, it is useful to offer a somewhat more descriptive analysis of the locational changes in three industries that have had an important presence in the Rust Belt: steel, motor vehicles, and rubber tires. These three have formed the core of the manufacturing sector from Pittsburgh to Milwaukee for at least seventy-five years. Each has begun to move southward in the past two decades, and this movement is likely to continue for the foreseeable future.

## Steel

The U.S. steel industry has suffered a mammoth restructuring since the mid-1970s. In the popular press, this restructuring has been ascribed to excess capacity and import competition, but one of the most important causes has been the growth in the new, smaller minimill companies that have replaced the less efficient, large integrated steelmakers in many product lines.[1]

The steel industry reached its record output in 1973, shipping 111 million tons of finished steel. Between 1973 and 1982, the industry's output fell by a startling 45 percent as the economy suffered its worst recession since the 1930s. Steel output peaked once again in 1990, but the 1990 peak was more than 26 million tons below the 1973 peak because of a decline in U.S. steel consumption of 25 million tons and an increase in net imports of 2 million tons (table

1. Donald F. Barnett and Robert W. Crandall, *Up from the Ashes: The Rise of the Steel Minimill in the United States* (Brookings, 1986).

**Table 5-1. U.S. Steel Shipments, Imports, and Consumption, 1970–91**
Millions of tons

| Year | Shipments | Imports | Apparent consumption[a] |
|------|-----------|---------|------------------------|
| 1970 | 90.8 | 13.4 | 97.1 |
| 1971 | 87.0 | 18.3 | 102.5 |
| 1972 | 91.8 | 17.7 | 106.6 |
| 1973 | 111.4 | 15.2 | 122.5 |
| 1974 | 109.5 | 16.0 | 119.6 |
| 1975 | 80.0 | 12.0 | 89.0 |
| 1976 | 89.4 | 14.3 | 101.1 |
| 1977 | 91.1 | 19.3 | 108.5 |
| 1978 | 97.9 | 21.1 | 116.6 |
| 1979 | 100.3 | 17.5 | 115.0 |
| 1980 | 83.9 | 15.5 | 95.2 |
| 1981 | 88.5 | 19.9 | 105.4 |
| 1982 | 61.6 | 16.7 | 76.4 |
| 1983 | 67.6 | 17.1 | 83.5 |
| 1984 | 73.7 | 26.2 | 98.9 |
| 1985 | 73.0 | 24.3 | 96.4 |
| 1986 | 70.3 | 20.7 | 90.0 |
| 1987 | 76.7 | 20.4 | 95.9 |
| 1988 | 83.8 | 20.9 | 102.7 |
| 1989 | 84.1 | 17.3 | 96.8 |
| 1990 | 85.0 | 17.2 | 97.8 |
| 1991 | 78.8 | 15.8 | 88.3 |

Source: American Iron and Steel Institute, *Annual Statistical Reports* (Washington: AISI, various years).
a. Domestic shipments minus exports plus imports.

5-1). In the 1980s, average steel consumption was 94 million tons; in the 1970s, it had been 108 million tons.

The decline in steel consumption was exacerbated by the rise in the value of the dollar in the first half of the 1980s. The resultant surge in imports, combined with sluggish overall demand for steel and the growth in minimills, forced the large integrated steel companies to retrench (table 5-2). These large companies, such as Bethlehem, Inland, and U.S. Steel, use blast furnaces, coke ovens, and large basic-oxygen steelmaking furnaces to transform iron ore into molten steel. Their high labor costs, the product of generous collective bargaining agreements in the 1970s and low productivity, made them increasingly noncompetitive with the smaller minimills that melt scrap in electric furnaces, particularly for the small-diameter products. As a result, minimills added nearly 20 million tons of capacity between 1975 and 1989 while the large integrated firms shed more than 50 million tons.

**Table 5-2. U.S. Raw Steel Capacity, Selected Years, 1965–89**
Millions of tons

| Year | Integrated firms[a] | Minimills | Total |
|------|---------------------|-----------|-------|
| 1965 | 143.7 | 4.5 | 148.2 |
| 1970 | 146.3 | 7.5 | 153.8 |
| 1975 | 142.9 | 10.2 | 153.1 |
| 1980 | 138.2 | 15.5 | 153.7 |
| 1985 | 111.8 | 21.8 | 133.6 |
| 1989 | 89.2 | 29.0 | 118.2 |

Sources: American Iron and Steel Institute, *Annual Statistical Reports*; Donald F. Barnett and Robert W. Crandall, *Up from the Ashes: The Rise of the Steel Minimill in the United States* (Brookings, 1986), p. 12 (updated by the author).
a. Includes specialty steel firms that produce stainless and alloy products.

Most of the integrated companies' capacity reduction was in the Northeast and Great Lakes states, but plants were also closed or sold in California and Texas (see table 5-3).[2] Besides the plant closures listed in the table, many other Rust Belt steel plants were downsized as demand weakened and the integrated firms found that they could no longer compete with the minimills in steel bars, wire rods, small structural shapes, and concrete reinforcing bars.

The newer minimill companies can build capacity at $250 to $300 per ton of raw steel, while a new integrated works is estimated to cost as much as $1,400 per ton of capacity.[3] Only two integrated plants have been built in the United States since World War II; the last was Bethlehem's northern Indiana plant, which was completed in the late 1960s. More than thirty new minimills have been built since 1970, and more are likely to be built in the 1990s.

At first, minimill producers attacked the markets for the lower-grade, small-diameter bar and rod products, but recently they have moved into higher-quality and larger bar and structural products and even sheet products. As the minimills advanced from making simple reinforcing bars to making higher-quality bars, rods, and structural shapes, the integrated firms' only choice was to retreat from these markets and to close facilities because of the minimills' very large cost advantages. These advantages derive from low real prices of scrap, lower unit labor costs, lower plant costs, and fewer plant layout constraints. The minimills' labor costs are lower largely

2. Some facilities continue to operate at a few of the plants listed in table 5-3, but the basic steelmaking capacity has been closed in all listed plants. USX closed its Utah plant and later sold it. It now operates as Geneva Steel.

3. Barnett and Crandall, *Up from the Ashes*, pp. 53, 65.

**Table 5-3. Integrated Firms' Steel Plants Closed since 1976**

| Plant and location | Capacity (millions of raw tons) | Plant and location | Capacity (millions of raw tons) |
|---|---|---|---|
| Alan Wood | | U.S. Steel | |
|   Conshohocken, Pa. | 1.2 |   Baytown, Tex. | 1.5 |
| Armco | |   Fairless, Pa. | 1.8 |
|   Houston, Tex. | 1.0 |   Duquesne, Pa. | 2.4 |
| Bethlehem | |   South Chicago, Ill. | 3.8 |
|   Lackawanna, N.Y. | 2.6 |   Youngstown, Ohio | 2.0 |
| CF&I | | Wheeling-Pittsburgh | |
|   Pueblo, Colo. | 1.2 |   Monessen, Pa. | 1.5 |
| Jones & Laughlin | | Wisconsin Steel | |
|   Aliquippa, Pa. | 4.4 |   South Chicago, Ill. | 1.1 |
|   Pittsburgh, Pa. | 1.9 | Youngstown Sheet & Tube | |
| Kaiser Steel | |   Youngstown, Ohio | 3.4 |
|   Fontana, Calif. | 3.3 | Regions | |
| Republic Steel | |   Middle Atlantic | 16.5 |
|   Chicago, Ill. | 1.1 |   East north central | 11.4 |
|   Buffalo, N.Y. | 0.9 |   South | 2.5 |
| | |   West | 4.5 |
| | |   Total closures | 35.1 |

Source: American Iron and Steel Institute, *Annual Statistical Reports.*

because of much higher productivity but not necessarily because of lower compensation per hour. Because minimills often tie their compensation to output, their workers are much more productive than those in the older integrated facilities.[4]

The minimill companies have located most of their new facilities in the South, but there are numerous exceptions (see table 5-4). A Canadian minimill company, CoSteel, built a large wire-rod plant in New Jersey in the late 1970s. Another smaller minimill producing lower-quality reinforcing bars was also built in New Jersey in the 1970s. In the late 1980s, Nucor built in central Indiana the first U.S. minimill designed to produce sheet steel. A few other plants have been built in Pennsylvania, Rhode Island, and New York, but

4. In addition, the integrated firms have agreed to extremely expensive early-retirement provisions in their union contracts that not only reduce work incentives but also make it very difficult to close their older plants. These provisions often require the companies to record additional expenditures per employee with a present value of $100,000 or more upon the closure of a plant. The closure of one large plant employing 5,000 workers would bankrupt all but two of the remaining companies.

**Table 5-4. Raw Steel Capacity of Minimills Built since 1970, by Region**
Millions of tons

| Region | Capacity |
|---|---|
| New England | 300 |
| Middle Atlantic | 2,420 |
| East north central | 2,280 |
| West north central | 880 |
| South | 8,030 |
| West | 700 |
| Total | 14,610 |

Source: Metal Bulletin, *Iron and Steel Works of the World*, 9th ed. (Surrey, England: Metal Bulletin Books, 1987).

**Table 5-5. The Shift in U.S. Raw Steel Production, 1973–90**
Millions of tons

| Region | 1973 | 1990 | Change |
|---|---|---|---|
| Northeast[a] | 47.9 | 17.2 | − 30.7 |
| Midwest | 74.5 | 53.9 | − 20.6 |
| South | 13.3 | 15.8 | 2.5 |
| Plains[b] | 5.6 | 6.6 | 1.0 |
| West | 9.5 | 5.4 | − 4.1 |
| Total | 150.8 | 98.9 | − 51.9 |

Source: American Iron and Steel Institute, *Annual Statistical Reports*.
a. Includes a very small amount of capacity in New England.
b. Includes Texas.

more than half the new minimill capacity has been built in the South.

The combined effect of integrated closures and new minimill additions has led to a shift of U.S. steelmaking to the South (table 5-5). Industry statistics show that between 1973 and 1990, raw steel production fell by 51 million tons in the Rust Belt, a decline of 42 percent. In the same period, steelmaking actually increased in the South and in the Plains states (including Texas) despite the 34 percent decline in total U.S. output. The most stunning decline was registered by the northeastern states—particularly New York and Pennsylvania, whose share fell from 32 percent of U.S. raw steel output to 17 percent. Census data generally corroborate these trends (table 5-6). Between 1967 and 1977, the middle Atlantic and east north central regions maintained their 75 percent share of the steel industry's employment and value added. Between 1977 and 1987, however, the middle Atlantic states lost nearly 10 percentage points of their share of output and employment while the east north

**Table 5-6. The Share of U.S. Steel Manufacture in Middle Atlantic and East North Central Regions, Selected Years, 1967–87**

Percent

|  | Employment | | | Value added | | |
|---|---|---|---|---|---|---|
| Region | 1967 | 1977 | 1987 | 1967 | 1977 | 1987 |
| Middle Atlantic | 35.3 | 30.2 | 22.5 | 33.4 | 28.0 | 18.5 |
| East north central | 39.6 | 41.8 | 45.8 | 42.1 | 47.7 | 50.9 |

Source: Bureau of the Census, *Census of Manufactures*, "Geographic Area Studies" (Department of Commerce, 1967, 1977, 1987).

central states realized an increase of 3 to 4 percent of sharply declining national output and employment. However, the east north central region is likely to lose a substantial share of its output in the next decade.

The reasons for the regional shift in steelmaking are not difficult to discern. First, the switch to electric furnaces has led to the substitution of virtually ubiquitous ferrous scrap for iron ore and metallurgical coal, which are found principally in Canada and the northern and Appalachian states. As a result, the Great Lakes states, Pennsylvania, and upstate New York have lost their locational advantages.

Second, a large share of the new minimills have been built in southern states that have low unionization rates, often because of right-to-work laws. Virtually all of the integrated firms are unionized. Thus the growth of minimills is in large part a substitution of nonunion plants for the older unionized plants of the integrated firms.

Third, as has been shown, steel-consuming durable-goods industries have moved steadily southward and westward. In addition, commercial construction has grown more rapidly in the South and West than in the rest of the country. Given the relatively low value of steel per unit weight, transportation costs are an important factor in the location decision for steel production. As a result, some of the largest new minimills are in the South and West, such as Chaparral's Texas plant, Nucor's two new Arkansas plants, Georgetown's South Carolina plant, Cascade's Oregon plant, Oregon Steel's Portland plant, and North Star's Texas plant.

Fourth, minimills require large amounts of electrical energy rather than metallurgical coal. As a result, they are most likely to locate in states with relatively low industrial electricity rates. States such as Arkansas, Louisiana, South Carolina, Nebraska, Oregon, Washington, and Utah—all with substantial recent minimill investment—have electricity rates that are generally below the average U.S. rate.[5]

Finally, the large share of integrated steel manufacture that remains in the Great Lakes area is almost entirely devoted to the manufacture of sheet products. Because minimills have invaded these sheet products only recently, these integrated Great Lakes plants continue to dominate the market for sheet products, which account for nearly 50 percent of the U.S. steel market. However, this dominance is now being threatened by minimills employing the new technology for casting thin slabs.

As with the manufacturing sector in general, there is very little indication that the migration of steel production has begun to slow. Northern integrated plants continue to close. The most recent examples are U.S. Steel's 1991 decision to close its eastern Pennsylvania (Fairless) plant and Sharon's closure in early 1993. A few of the older plants have been revived after having been spun off from the larger companies, but even these have uncertain futures at best. Weirton Steel (West Virginia), Gadsden Steel (Alabama), Geneva Steel (Utah), and Warren Consolidated Industries (Ohio) are the best examples of these reconstituted mills. Two of these four integrated plants that have been given at least a temporary lease on life are in the South and West. Moreover, U.S. Steel has invested substantial amounts in its Fairfield (Alabama) and Pittsburg (California) works.[6] Thus, even in the case of integrated works, the direction is gently southward and westward.

More ominously, Nucor has recently built a second sheet-steel plant in Arkansas using the same technology for thin slab casting that it first introduced in its Indiana plant. At first, each of these plants was designed to produce only 1 million tons a year, far below the minimum efficient scale of the older, integrated process (3 million to 5 million tons a year). Each of these new plants may eventually produce 2 million tons a year, and although they will account

5. See Energy Information Administration, *State Energy Price and Expenditure Report, 1988* (Department of Energy, September 1990).

6. The Pittsburg works is now a joint venture between USX and Korea's Pohang Steel. This plant is simply a finishing facility, not a fully integrated plant.

for only about 8 percent of U.S. sheet-steel output, they reflect a major intrusion by minimills into the last bastion of integrated steel company strength. In 1993 Nucor announced that it will build a third sheet-steel plant—as a joint venture with Oregon Steel—in the Pacific region.

Nucor's success in producing sheet products has led to a flurry of activity among other U.S. producers. North Star and Chaparral have been actively looking for sites to build similar sheet plants in the South. Two Canadian firms also will build a plant in the United States. U.S. Steel may be the first integrated firm to build a minimill sheet plant in the mid-South using an even more revolutionary strip-casting technology.[7]

By 2000, there will probably be 10 million to 20 million tons of minimill sheet capacity. Most of this capacity will simply replace existing integrated capacity. National Steel's St. Louis plant, U.S. Steel's Monongahela Valley works, Armco's Ashland (Kentucky) plant, and a variety of marginal facilities in western Pennsylvania and eastern Ohio are candidates for closure in the next decade. The new minimill plants will undoubtedly be concentrated in the Ohio and Mississippi valleys far from the unionized environment of northern Ohio, Pennsylvania, Illinois, and Indiana. The shift of steel from the Rust Belt has thus only just begun.

It was the steel industry that was the very symbol of the Rust Belt, relying on iron ore from Minnesota and Canada and metallurgical coal from Appalachia. However, the absence of growth in steel demand, the shift of steel markets to the South and West, and the growth of minimills has all but devastated most of the old steel-producing areas in the Rust Belt. There are no integrated steel works left in Youngstown, Ohio, and the one that remains in Warren, Ohio, is marginal at best. All of the raw steelmaking facilities in Buffalo, New York, have been closed. Even in the Pittsburgh area, once the center of the U.S. steel industry, only one integrated works remains.

The Rust Belt steel-making regions that have survived as steel-producing centers—the South Chicago–Northern Indiana, Detroit, and Cleveland areas—have lost substantial capacity in the last fifteen years. At present, they depend almost entirely on the automotive market, which is slowly moving southward. Indeed, even

7. Dana Milbank, "U.S. Steel Plans Strategy Shift with Minimill," *Wall Street Journal*, August 5, 1992, p. 3.

these steel plants will continue to reduce capacity over the next decade as minimills built elsewhere take more and more of the sheet steel market from them.

## Motor Vehicles

Like the steel industry, the motor vehicle industry concentrated about 75 percent of its output and employment in the Rust Belt through the 1960s. The early pioneers—Ford, Durant, and Chrysler—located their plants in southern Michigan. As in the steel industry, the large vehicle producers have been steadily losing market share to newcomers—in this case, to foreign producers. At first, this loss was to imports from Europe; after 1973, however, it was to imports from Japan. By 1980, Japanese imports had risen to nearly 25 percent of the U.S. market. U.S. motor vehicle companies lost $4.3 billion in 1980 after earning $4.6 billion in 1979.[8] And by 1980 industry employment had fallen by 200,000 from its 1978 level, creating strong domestic pressure for import quotas.

In 1981 the Reagan administration negotiated the first voluntary restraint agreements (VRAs) with the Japanese, limiting Japanese imports to 1.68 million passenger cars a year. These quotas were raised to 1.85 million cars in 1984 and subsequently to 2.3 million cars, where they remained through 1991.[9] As a result of these trade barriers, the Japanese began to invest heavily in U.S. motor vehicle production facilities in the 1980s. Honda, anticipating future trade friction, made its decision in 1978 to build a plant in central Ohio, which opened in 1982. By 1990 every major Japanese automobile producer except Daihatsu had initiated production in the United States, some as joint venture partners and others by themselves.

There are now eight Japanese "transplant" assembly complexes in the United States. Four are owned outright by one of the three major Japanese companies: Honda, Nissan, and Toyota. Two are joint ventures with U.S. producers: Toyota-General Motors (NUMMI) in Fremont, California, and Chrysler-Mitsubishi (Dia-

8. Bureau of Economic Analysis, *Income and Product Accounts of the United States*, vol. 2: *1959–88* (Department of Commerce, September 1992), table 6-16C.

9. The VRAs were tightened in 1992, but are probably not binding, given the decline in the dollar and the growth in Japanese-owned assembly plants in the United States.

**Table 5-7. Regional Shares of Passenger Car Assembly, Selected Years, 1965–90**

Percent

| Region | 1965 | 1970 | 1975 | 1980 | 1984 | 1990 |
|---|---|---|---|---|---|---|
| Northeast | 10.3 | 8.4 | 9.0 | 16.9 | 8.7 | 3.7 |
| East north central | 49.9 | 49.6 | 54.2 | 46.4 | 51.6 | 58.3 |
| West north central | 14.1 | 14.8 | 13.3 | 10.3 | 16.4 | 9.7 |
| South | 16.4 | 18.9 | 16.6 | 21.4 | 20.4 | 23.1 |
| West | 9.3 | 8.3 | 6.8 | 5.0 | 2.9 | 5.2 |
| Total | 100.0 | 100.0 | 99.9 | 100.0 | 100.0 | 100.0 |

Source: Motor Vehicle Manufacturers Association of the United States, *Motor Vehicle Facts and Figures* (Detroit: MVMA, various years).

mond Star) in Normal, Illinois.[10] Mazda, in which Ford has a major equity interest, opened a plant in Flat Rock, Michigan, to produce Mazdas and Ford Probes. Most recently, Subaru and Isuzu opened a joint-venture assembly plant in Lafayette, Indiana.

The locational choices for each of these transplant facilities appear to differ little from the existing geographical distribution of motor vehicle assembly in the United States. Table 5-7 shows the distribution of passenger car assembly by census region over the past twenty-five years. The combined share of assembly occurring in the east north central and northeast regions has remained in the range of 58 to 63 percent over the entire period. The West (California) has lost share to the South, but otherwise there is surprisingly little change in geographical location, given the enormous change that has occurred in other metal and metal-fabricating industries.

The reasons for this stability appear to be related to industrial relations and the location of input-supplying industries. The U.S. motor vehicle industry has been dominated by the Big Three producers: General Motors, Ford, and Chrysler. All of these firms' production facilities are totally unionized,[11] and each firm has signed labor contracts that include increasing degrees of employment protection. As a practical matter, these companies cannot build non-union plants in the South or West, but they also face stiff penalties from permanent closures of plants unless they reemploy the workers in other facilities. The result of these contracts is to induce the firms

10. Chrysler recently sold its interest in Diamond Star to Mitsubishi.

11. Even General Motors' new Saturn plant in Tennessee is organized by the United Auto Workers.

to renovate existing plants or to build new ones close to those that are permanently shut.

Since the late 1970s, General Motors has been the only Big Three company to build many new assembly plants. Chrysler built two new plants in Michigan while closing two others in Michigan and one in Wisconsin that it acquired when it bought American Motors. Ford has rebuilt several plants, but it has not built a new assembly plant in more than a decade. General Motors, however, has built eight new assembly plants. Two of these plants were built in Michigan, two were built in the mid-South,[12] two in the Southwest, and one each in Missouri, Kansas, and Louisiana. But it also closed three plants in Michigan, two in Missouri, three in California, and one each in Ohio, Georgia, Kansas, and Massachusetts. Thus its movement has been slightly southward, but it has greatly reduced West Coast production.

The regional pattern of transplant investment is very similar to that of the Big Three. The only western plant built by the new players has been the Toyota-GM joint venture (NUMMI) at General Motors' old plant site in Fremont, California. The other joint U.S.-Japanese ventures have been built in the Detroit area and Normal, Illinois. All of the independent Japanese plants have been built within one hundred miles of a straight line drawn between Nashville, Tennessee, and Detroit. Thus, the transplants and General Motors have moved the center of the industry slightly southward but not westward.

The census data on employment and value added in the motor vehicle industry (SIC 371) show a substantial decline for the east north central and mid-Atlantic states between 1977 and 1987 (table 5-8). In 1977 the east north central and middle Atlantic states accounted for 71 percent of motor vehicle industry value added and 73 percent of industry employment. By 1987 these shares had fallen to 63 and 65 percent, respectively. But these data fail to capture much of the recent growth in transplant production. The continued growth of Honda in Ohio and new transplant operations in Michigan, Indiana, and Illinois will not only limit the decline of the midwestern motor vehicle industry, but may even expand its share of industry employment and output.

---

12. The Saturn plant in Tennessee has been staffed almost entirely from workers drawn from other GM facilities, primarily in the North.

**Table 5-8. The Share of U.S. Motor Vehicle Manufacture in Middle Atlantic and East North Central Regions, Selected Years, 1967–87**
Percent

| | Employment | | | Value added | | |
|---|---|---|---|---|---|---|
| Region | 1967 | 1977 | 1987 | 1967 | 1977 | 1987 |
| Middle Atlantic | 8.6[a] | 9.1[a] | 8.1 | 8.8[a] | 7.9[a] | 6.4 |
| East north central | 68.1 | 63.5 | 56.5[a] | 66.3 | 62.9 | 56.4[a] |

Source: Bureau of the Census, *Census of Manufactures*, "Geographic Area Studies" (Department of Commerce, 1967, 1977, 1987).
a. Estimated by author.

The apparent stability in the midwestern share of motor vehicle production is quite consistent with the findings in chapter 2. First, the transplant operations in Ohio and Indiana are nonunion. Honda's Marysville, East Liberty, and Anna plants are located in generally rural central Ohio in labor markets that resemble Tennessee or Kentucky more than Detroit or Cleveland. Second, the Big Three's continued attachment to traditional Rust Belt locations is not an unconstrained choice, given their existing union contracts. Their failure to close their facilities and to move southward is consistent with the result in chapter 2 that unionization is also inversely related to contractions or closures. The Big Three have been in a phase of contraction (with the exception of Ford).

Thus, like the integrated steel industry, the motor vehicle industry is maintaining a large share of its regional base in the Midwest. It is shifting southward very slowly from the Great Lakes to central Ohio, Indiana, Illinois, Tennessee, and Kentucky. Heavily dependent on outside suppliers of steel, glass, and components and shifting rapidly to "just-in-time" production techniques, the new players are reluctant to move very far from the old centers of flat-rolled steel and parts production. Moreover, the Japanese transplants that are not joint ventures have been universally successful in avoiding union organization, regardless of whether they are in heavily unionized states such as Ohio or Indiana or in right-to-work states such as Kentucky and Tennessee.

## The Tire Industry

There is perhaps no American manufacturing industry that has undergone more revolutionary changes in the past thirty years than the rubber tire industry. In the 1960s, six U.S. producers controlled nearly 75 percent of the industry's output. Most plants were located in the Rust Belt. Indeed, more than half of industry employment was in the northeast or east north central regions. By 1991, five of the six U.S. major producers no longer existed as independent entities. Foreign producers—such as Dunlop, Michelin, Pirelli, Continental, Bridgestone, and Yokohama—now own about 60 percent of U.S. production capacity, much of it acquired through merger. Many plants in the Great Lakes and Northeast have closed, reducing employment and capacity in these regions to about 20 percent.[13]

One of the reasons for the dramatic shift in ownership in the industry has been the change in tire technology. In the 1950s and 1960s, the major U.S. companies produced mostly bias-ply tires. The foreign producers, such as Michelin and Pirelli, were among the leaders in radial-tire technology. As the U.S. market began to demand radial tires in the 1970s, principally because of their contribution to vehicle fuel efficiency, the U.S. producers found themselves at a competitive disadvantage. One company, Firestone, had a disastrous experience with its first radial passenger tire that nearly bankrupted the company.

Even before the foreign producers began to acquire a large share of U.S. capacity, the industry had begun to migrate southward. In 1967, 24 percent of industry employment was in the South; by 1977 this share had doubled. The regional migration continued throughout the 1970s and 1980s. In 1976, 48 percent of tire capacity was in the South; by 1991 the South's share was about 75 percent. The Rust Belt states, which accounted for two-thirds of the industry in the 1960s, retained only about 20 percent of industry capacity.[14]

Less than 25 percent of the industry's output is represented by original-equipment shipments to vehicle assemblers; hence the industry is less hostage to the location of motor vehicle assembly plants than is the flat-rolled steel industry. As a result, one might expect regional input prices to be more important in tire plant location than in the steel industry. Moreover, the tire industry is less tied to old plants than is the steel industry. Because new plants can

13. "Estimated Tire Plant Capabilities," *Modern Tire Dealer*, January 1991, pp. 34–35.

14. Perhaps the most stunning indication of the Rust Belt's loss of tire production is the absence of any capacity in Akron, Ohio, once the "Rubber Capital" of the country. Data on industry capacity are available in the January editions of *Modern Tire Dealer*, 1976–present.

be built economically, many have been. Indeed, the enormous shift of capacity from North to South is largely the result of new plant openings and older plant closings, not simply plant expansions and contractions.

The effects of variables such as wage rates, tax rates, unionization, and energy prices on plant location can be determined by estimating a distributed-lag equation,

$$(5\text{-}1) \quad CAP_t = f(CAP_{t-1}, WAGERATE, UNION, ENERGY, TAX, \\ INFRA, GOVT),$$

over the period 1976–91 where $CAP$ is daily tire capacity and the other variables are as defined in chapter 2. (Earlier capacity data by state are not available.) The results, not surprisingly, show that labor market variables are important, but that taxes, energy prices, and infrastructure are not. These results, excluding the *INFRA*, *GOVT*, and *UNION* variables, are (*t*-statistics shown in parentheses):

$$(5\text{-}1a) \quad CAP_{91} = 108.8 + 0.70 \, CAP_{76} - 17.12 \, WAGERATE$$
$$\phantom{(5\text{-}1a) \quad CAP_{91} = 108.8} (6.22) \phantom{+ 0.70 \, CAP_{76} -} (3.57)$$

$$- 4.64 \, ENERGY - 7.42 \, TAX.$$
$$\phantom{-} (0.69) \phantom{\, ENERGY -} (1.03)$$
$$\bar{R}^2 = 0.487; \, n = 48$$

Similar results obtain when *UNION* is substituted for *WAGE-RATE*, once again reflecting the collinearity of unionization and wage rates. Thus it appears that capacity is shifting to low-wage, nonunion states, but that taxes and energy costs are less important in explaining the southern drift of tire capacity.

## Conclusion

The heart of the steel, tire, and motor vehicle industries is no longer to be found in the 200 miles from Pittsburgh to Detroit. Each of these industries has moved southward and to a much lesser extent westward over the past twenty-five years. This movement is not primarily a reflection of established firms closing old northern plants and opening glistening new ones in the South or West. Rather, it is part of an evolution in which new firms are taking markets away from older companies that are slow to innovate and are tied to out-dated forms of industrial relations.

The tire industry is perhaps the best example of this transformation. Of the major U.S. tire companies in the 1960s, only Goodyear remains as an independent U.S. entity. As the U.S. companies faltered in their northern locations, they opened new plants in the South and Southwest. However, the competition from Michelin, Pirelli, Bridgestone, and other foreign firms eventually proved irresistible, and the U.S. companies sold out one by one to these foreign rivals, leading to further plant rationalizations. The result is that a very large share of tire production has now shifted to lower-wage, nonunion plants in the South.

The steel industry has gone through a similar evolution except that its competitors are small domestic firms who have no interest in buying the dying industry dinosaurs. As a result, a large number of the large steel companies have entered Chapter 11 bankruptcy proceedings and have sharply reduced their capacity.[15] Given the large sunk costs in this industry, exit is painfully slow, but it is a safe prediction that this exit will continue as northern integrated plants close while numerous new southern or southwestern minimill plants replace them.

The replacement rate in the motor vehicle industry is the slowest of the three under consideration in this chapter. The Big Three U.S. producers still account for about 60 percent of U.S. industry sales, a share that has been artificially bolstered by a bailout of Chrysler in 1979 and trade protection since 1981. In addition, the Japanese companies were dissuaded from expanding their transplant activities in the United States in the early 1990s. Finally, because of brand loyalty, market shares change more slowly in motor vehicles than in steel or even rubber tires. Despite these impediments, there can be little doubt that the motor vehicle industry is going through the same transition that has gripped steel and tires. New players are replacing decades-old firms and steadily moving the industry southward. The old firms, locked into labor agreements and northern plants, have little room to maneuver and are slowly, inexorably yielding to new, more efficient firms with superior industrial relations.

15. These include Alan Wood, Wisconsin Steel, CF&I, Sharon Steel, Wheeling-Pittsburgh, McLouth, and LTV. LTV Steel, in turn, is the product of mergers among Youngstown Sheet & Tube, Republic, and Jones & Laughlin. Thus nine integrated steel companies have either landed in bankruptcy court or have simply disappeared.

*Chapter Six*

# The Role of Government in the Migration of Industry

THERE IS CONSIDERABLE skepticism among students of business location as to the wisdom of using government incentives to stimulate local or regional business activity. This skepticism reflects both an unease about the robustness of the empirical evidence supporting any particular incentive—such as tax reductions or targeted expenditures—and a fear that the cost of these incentives to current members of communities exceeds their benefits.

Despite these doubts, many state and local governments continue to offer specific tax incentives, improvements in infrastructure, or targeted spending on education or other services in an effort to increase local employment. In addition, there is recurring interest in a national industrial policy, particularly in areas that have been losing manufacturing employment. As the United States reduces the size of its defense sector, the demand for such industrial policies is likely to grow. In this chapter, I provide a concluding assessment on possible government policies designed to slow the shifts in the U.S. manufacturing base.

## Regional versus Intraregional Shifts in the Manufacturing Base

The focus in this study has been on the shift of industry from the North to the South and West. But manufacturing activity moves within regions, within states, and—indeed—even within metropolitan areas. The decline of large northern central cities and its attendant effects upon the underclass, for example, may be more a function of the flight to suburbia than of the migration of industry

96

southward and westward.[1] Thus one has to be careful to specify the dimensions of the regional change being examined before looking for its causes or for potential policies to slow or reverse it.

The effects of tax rates, government spending, infrastructure, factor prices, and other variables on plant location decisions generally vary with the set of geographical choices being analyzed. For this reason, students of state and local development policies are careful to distinguish the results of *intra*state or *intra*-area studies from those of *inter*state studies.[2] Locational choices within a state or a metropolitan area are more likely to be affected by local tax rates or government expenditures than are choices across states or regions.

An example of the importance of geographic focus may be seen in the study by Bartik and his colleagues of the choice of locations for General Motors' Saturn plant.[3] They examined a small number of locations extending only as far south as Nashville, as far west as St. Louis, and as far north as Kalamazoo. Because General Motors is locked into a union contract, the wages at the assembly plant would not vary with locational choice, but local suppliers' wage rates would vary across the various locations. Despite this constraint, the range of labor costs per car across the locations—as reflected only in suppliers' component prices—was somewhat greater than the range in state and local taxes for the plant. The final choice, Nashville, was the lowest labor-cost area studied and nearly the lowest state and local tax jurisdiction of those studied.

The choice of location by General Motors was limited to the Midwest and mid-South because of the logistics of parts supply and the company's UAW contract. Given this array of choices, its choice of Tennessee might have been influenced by relative tax rates. However, had General Motors been less constrained, it might have chosen to look more widely and make a final choice driven much more by labor costs than by taxes, infrastructure, or local government spending.[4]

1. Mark Alan Hughes with Julie E. Sternberg, *The New Metropolitan Reality: Where the Rubber Meets the Road in Antipoverty Policy* (Washington: Urban Institute, 1992).

2. See, for example, the survey by Timothy J. Bartik, *Who Benefits from State and Local Economic Development Policies?* (Kalamazoo: W. E. Upjohn Institute for Employment Research, 1991), app. 2.2–app. 2.5.

3. Timothy J. Bartik and others, "Saturn and State Economic Development," *Forum for Applied Research and Public Policy*, vol. 2 (Spring 1987), pp. 29–41.

4. It is possible that at the location finally chosen, near Nashville, infrastructure investments by the state (in highways) may have had some effect on General Motors'

## Competition among Jurisdictions

The absence of a clear effect of state and local government policy instruments in many of the studies of interstate locational choice may seem counterintuitive, given the efforts that governments expend to attract manufacturing plants. One would expect the effects to be significant in light of the tax concessions and specific infrastructure expenditures often underwritten to attract these businesses.

There are at least two reasons why the effects of state and local tax or expenditure policies may be muted in empirical studies of regional growth. First, use of generally applicable tax rates or expenditures in regression analyses may fail to capture specific concessions to manufacturers seeking to locate new plants. Second, differences in these concessions and even in general tax rates across states may be constrained by interstate (or intermetropolitan area) competition for new plants. As a result, the differences in taxes may be dominated by large differences in labor costs or other input costs across states or regions.[5]

Obviously, any general differences in property, sales, or corporate taxes across jurisdictions can be narrowed by competition for specific new plants. States and municipalities can and will bid for large new industrial plants, particularly those promising substantial demand for local labor, by offering a variety of tax concessions or specific investments. These concessions are likely to be unreported, leading to spurious reports of major tax differences as the determining factor in the final choice of location.

On the other hand, a state's attempts to improve the quality of its labor force or the quality of life that attracts a highly skilled labor force

---

final decision. A more recent study on branch plant location in the motor vehicle industry finds that labor market variables are insignificant, but the authors suggest that this result undoubtedly reflects the fact that most companies in the sample are already unionized and cannot benefit from low-wage, nonunion locations. See Virginia D. McConnell and Robert M. Schwab, "The Impact of Environmental Regulation on Industry Location Decisions: The Motor Vehicle Industry," *Land Economics*, vol. 66 (February 1990), pp. 67–81.

5. For an insightful critique of the methodology employed in many studies of tax rates on business location, see Robert J. Newman and Dennis H. Sullivan, "Econometric Analysis of Business Tax Impacts on Industrial Location: What Do We Know, and How Do We Know It?" *Journal of Urban Economics*, vol. 23 (March 1988), pp. 215–34.

cannot be emulated easily. Investments in education, research parks, or expensive local amenities earn returns only after years or decades, and they may not succeed at all. Some studies have shown a sensitivity of business growth to expenditures by state and local governments on education.[6] The effect of research parks, however, appears only mildly related to their establishment, according to one recent study.[7] Finally, the success of "enterprise zones" in attracting new plants has not been investigated systematically in the literature. One recent study of Indiana's experience with enterprise zones concludes that they have succeeded in reducing unemployment in the designated areas, but have had the opposite effect on plant investment.[8]

## General Business Activity versus Manufacturing

Much of the empirical literature on locational decisions focuses on the entire nonfarm private economy. In these studies, government policy instruments appear to have much more effect than in studies focusing solely on the manufacturing sector or specific manufacturing industries. Indeed, a recent careful analysis of the effect of taxes on capital investment and new firm births in five three-digit manufacturing industries found that differences in the effective tax rate faced by firms in these industries had a negative effect in only three of the five industries, but the statistical significance of even these results was relatively low.[9] However, many recent studies of the effect of state and local taxes on measures of general business activity find a significantly negative effect.[10]

6. See Bartik, *Who Benefits*, app. 2.3, for a list of studies that included government expenditures on education, highways, and welfare. Education has a positive coefficient in a large share of the recent studies.

7. Breandan O hUallachain and Mark A. Satterthwaite, "Sectoral Growth Patterns at the Metropolitan Level: An Evaluation of Economic Development Incentives," *Journal of Urban Economics*, vol. 31 (January 1992), pp. 25–58.

8. Leslie E. Papke, "Tax Policy and Urban Development: Evidence from an Enterprise Program," Working Paper 3945 (Cambridge, Mass.: National Bureau of Economic Research, December 1991).

9. Leslie E. Papke, "The Responsiveness of Industrial Activity to Interstate Tax Differentials: A Comparison of Elasticities," in Henry W. Herzog, Jr., and Alan M. Schlottman, eds., *Industry Location and Public Policy* (University of Tennessee Press, 1991), pp. 120–34. Two earlier studies by Papke reach essentially the same conclusion.

10. Bartik, *Who Benefits*. See also Newman and Sullivan, "Econometric Analysis of Business Tax Impacts," for a somewhat skeptical view.

## Population Migration: The Lure of the Sun Belt

The Rust Belt developed because of its raw-material base and its proximity to the original population centers of the country. As the advantages of proximity to these raw materials dwindled and transportation and communications networks developed, northeastern locations began to lose their economic advantage. These conditions allowed population to migrate to more pleasant climates in the South and West. It does not require sophisticated economic analysis to understand why Florida, California, and Arizona have grown more rapidly than Pennsylvania, Michigan, and New York in recent decades. A simple climate variable explains a very large percentage of the variance in most models of total labor force growth or employment growth.

If people simply prefer to live in areas other than the traditional Rust Belt, any set of policies targeted toward manufacturing in these northern states is likely to have only modest effects in stemming the continued migration of industry. Under these conditions, it is also less likely that such policies can contribute to economic welfare in the long run. Rather than attempting to redistribute population from more desirable locations to less desirable locations, policies should be designed to ease the transitional difficulties caused by the sudden loss of employment in major industrial areas.

## Developing More Efficient Labor-Management Structures

The core industries of the Rust Belt for more than half a century were steel, rubber tires, and motor vehicles and parts. As I have discussed, each of these industries became a unionized oligopoly that atrophied badly and eventually encountered withering competition that it could not overcome. The regional shift in these industries was part of a larger phenomenon: the replacement of inefficient firms with high labor costs and poor product quality by new companies with lower labor costs and better product quality. Had it not been for trade protection in steel and motor vehicles and the government rescue of Chrysler, this transformation might have been more dramatic and perhaps relatively complete by today. Instead, the painful adjustment continues.

Any policy designed to prevent the flight of manufacturing to the Sun Belt is likely to reduce the competition provided by new firms with new plants. Indeed, much of the support for industrial policy comes from those desiring to protect declining firms and their employees. Unfortunately, such protection only entrenches the management and the industrial relations systems that have destroyed incentives for efficiency, innovation, and product quality. More than thirty years after the arrival of the Volkswagen Beetle in the United States and nearly twenty years after the first oil shock, the American automobile industry still appears on the verge of seeking protection from Japanese transplant operations.

These three industries are not the only concentrated durable-goods industries in which old-line firms have found it difficult to recover from years of poor performance without the external stimulus of competition from new entrants. In telephone equipment, for example, the entry of Northern Telecom and several European and Japanese suppliers has forced AT&T's former Western Electric manufacturing division to shed thousands of employees to remain competitive. After it lost virtually the entire market to Japanese producers (and after a brief period of trade protection), Harley David-son has finally been able to make a modest recovery in motorcycle manufacture.

Heavy equipment producers, such as Caterpillar and Cummins Engine, have been forced to undertake massive investment programs and employment reductions in order to survive in the competitive struggle with Japanese and European producers, some of whom have established production facilities in the United States. General Motors found it difficult to compete in large diesel engines and finally sold its diesel engine operation to a more entrepreneurial firm. Protected by a 25 percent tariff since the 1960s, U.S. heavy-truck manufacturers, such as White, General Motors, and Freightliner, began to fall behind their European counterparts. As a result, these U.S. producers have sold a large share of their operations to European producers, principally Volvo and Mercedes.

There are so many examples of large, durable-goods manufacturers in oligopolistic industries falling behind their world competitors in productive efficiency and product innovation that policymakers should worry about any general goal of maintaining the Rust Belt manufacturing base. As shown, the preference of new plants and expanding establishments for southern and western locations is at least mildly related to lower rates of unionization and lower wage rates in these regions. In many cases, these new and expanding plants reflect the decisions by Nucor, Toyota, Komatsu, or Northern Telecom to locate some distance from the industrial relations climate that is apparently suffocating their older, entrenched rivals. In virtually every case, the new plants have superior efficiency, lower labor costs, and higher product quality.

If the evolutionary process of industrial generation and regeneration is to continue in the United States, successful innovators must be allowed to replace those who are failing or have failed. A policy designed to keep manufacturing and its high-wage jobs in the North would undoubtedly have meant the perpetuation of inefficient management and labor practices in firms such as Firestone, Youngstown Sheet and Tube, Wisconsin Steel, Studebaker, Nash, or B. F. Goodrich. Slowing the migration of industry could hardly be accomplished without reducing the rate of new establishment formation, and reducing plant startups cannot be good for innovation and competitiveness.

## Some Possibilities for Regional Policy

There appears to be little harm in allowing states and municipalities to continue to compete for industry through the instruments they now use: tax concessions, targeted infrastructure investments, industrial parks, or even enterprise zones. Indeed, much more could be lost from attempting to stop such competition than from allowing it to run its course.

A substantial amount of U.S. environmental, health, and safety regulation exists precisely because of the notion that competition among the states in effecting their own policies is likely to result in both too little regulation and too many different regulatory standards. But nationalizing this type of regulation allows powerful national forces—industries and trade unions alike—to dictate its design. As a result, these national regulations are typically biased against smaller firms, nonunion firms, and new establishments.[11]

11. There is a very large literature on these effects. See, for example, Robert W. Crandall, *Controlling Industrial Pollution: The Economics and Politics of Clean Air* (Brookings, 1983); B. Peter Pashigian, "The Effect of Environmental Regulation on Optimal Plant Size and Factor Shares," *Journal of Law and Economics*, vol. 27 (April

One could hardly expect a uniform national "regional" policy to be any different.

The states might be encouraged, however, to proceed in at least two or three directions. First, they should design their policies to address the goal of providing productive, stable long-term employment for their labor force. This requires policies to stimulate labor demand when excess labor supply persists, not policies that induce a substitution of capital for labor. Because tax concessions typically reduce the before-tax return on capital required to justify building a new plant or reinvesting in an old one, they are more beneficial to capital-intensive than to labor-intensive activities. If insufficient demand for labor is the problem, a subsidy targeted at labor costs would be far more efficient than one that reduces corporate income taxes or property taxes. Some form of wage subsidy or forgiveness of employer contributions to mandatory state benefit programs would meet this requirement.

Second, a variety of state and local regulations may increase the cost of doing business, perhaps even in direct proportion to the number of workers employed. Most of these regulations, such as workmen's compensation, exist as the result of some state or local administrative or political process; therefore, they undoubtedly respond to a variety of pleadings from private interest groups. A major advantage of enterprise zones is the ability of government to suspend a large number of these regulations over a limited geographic domain without confronting each organized opposition group on each regulation. As mentioned above, there is relatively little careful empirical research on the effect of these enterprise zones on investment or employment, but they should at least be given a chance to work, particularly if regulations are adding substantially to the marginal cost of employing workers in areas of excess supply of labor.

Third, state and local governments should be encouraged to provide an environment in which human capital can develop. The principal conclusion of this study is that the decline of manufacturing in the Rust Belt is due to labor market conditions: high wages and a bad industrial relations environment. State and local governments can probably do little to affect the industrial relations environment

---

1984), pp. 1–28; and Ann P. Bartel and Lacy Glenn Thomas, "Direct and Indirect Effects of Regulation: A New Look at OSHA's Impact," *Journal of Law and Economics*, vol. 28 (April 1985), pp. 1–26.

directly. They can, however, at least attempt to improve public institutions of learning and provide a healthy environment for private ones. Whether targeted subsidies for training programs are likely to be productive in a rapidly changing industrial world is unclear, and an analysis of such subsidies is clearly beyond the scope of this study.

## Conclusion

The continuing migration of manufacturing industry toward the Sun Belt is not necessarily adverse to U.S. economic welfare, particularly if the population tends to view Sun Belt locations as better than those in the Rust Belt in providing environmental amenities. This migration may, however, create severe disruptions if it proceeds too rapidly or if it reflects reversible conditions in the Rust Belt. Both of these conditions may have been the case in areas such as Flint, Buffalo, or Akron, which lost a large share of their manufacturing base in a short period of time.

Unfortunately, there is little government can do to ameliorate the poor industrial relations climate created by decades of labor-management antagonism. It can, however, pursue policies that lower the incremental cost of employing labor or increase the human capital of local residents. Wage subsidies, reductions in employer contributions to government benefit programs, reduced regulation, or even enterprise zones might prove useful in offsetting the high cost of labor in some of these northern areas.

Mancur Olson has offered a theory on the decline of nations and regions within these nations.[12] The pursuit of special interest legislation or regulations designed to benefit one group at much greater cost to the overall society eventually succeeds. These government actions stifle growth and dissuade new investors, inducing them to look elsewhere. The result is a migration of industry to those regions or countries that are not yet affected by such policies. In Olson's theory, however, these newer regions eventually squander their initial advantage over the older regions through precisely the same

12. Mancur Olson, *The Rise and the Decline of Nations: Economic Growth, Stagflation, and Social Rigidities* (Yale University Press, 1982).

policies.[13] He has predicted that the North will rise again as the South and West atrophy from their own self-inflicted wounds. Perhaps he is correct, but as of 1993 there is no evidence that the shift in manufacturing is slowing. Northern states may eventually discover that it is in their interest to attempt to reduce impediments in their own labor markets. These policies may, in turn, slow the migration, but they seem unlikely to stop it.

13. Olson, "The South Will Fall Again: The South as Leader and Laggard in Economic Growth," *Southern Economic Journal*, vol. 49 (April 1983), pp. 917–32.

# Index